ONCE UPON A CLIMB

One Man's Journey on the Appalachian Trail

ONCE UPON A CLIMB

One Man's Journey on the Appalachian Trail

James "Reveille" Richardson

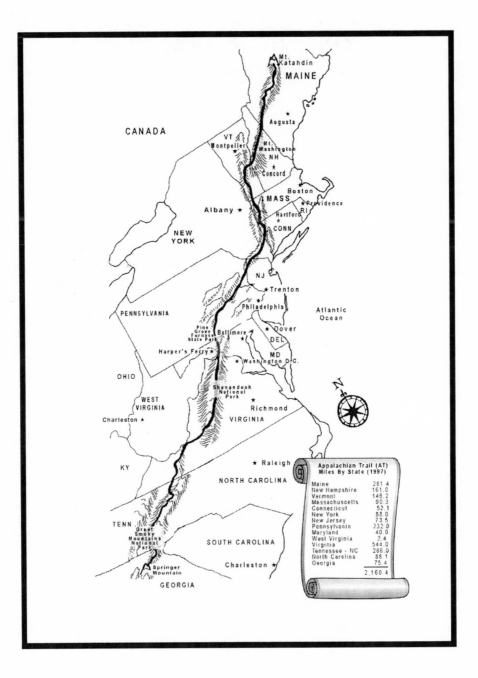

Mt. Katahdin

MAINE

CANADA

Augusta

VT
Montpelier
Mt. Washington
NH
Concord

Boston

MASS
Albany
Providence
RI
Hartford
CONN

NEW
YORK

NJ
Trenton

Philadelphia
Atlantic
Ocean

PENNSYLVANIA

Pine
Grove
Furnace
State Park
Baltimore
Dover
DEL

Harper's Ferry
MD
Washington D.C.

OHIO

WEST
VIRGINIA
Shenandoah
National
Park

Charleston
Richmond

VIRGINIA

KY
Raleigh

NORTH CAROLINA

TENN
Great
Smoky
Mountains
National
Park
SOUTH CAROLINA

Charleston

Springer
Mountain

GEORGIA

N

Appalachian Trail (AT)
Miles By State (1997)

Maine	281.4
New Hampshire	161.0
Vermont	146.2
Massachuscetts	90.3
Connecticut	52.1
New York	88.0
New Jersey	73.5
Pennsylvania	232.0
Maryland	40.0
West Virginia	2.4
Virginia	544.0
Tennessee - NC	286.0
North Carolina	88.1
Georgia	75.4
	2,160.4

DAY 1 – March 10, 1997. Trailhead at Amicalola Falls, Springer
Mountain, GA. Personal weight, 179 lb., pack weight, 53 lb.
Miles to go, 2,160.4.

CONTENTS

ACKNOWLEDGMENTS

First off, let me unequivocally state that no one thru-hikes the Appalachian Trail (AT) without a supporting cast. To paraphrase Hillary Clinton ... "It takes a village." For most, this support begins at home with family and significant others. They are there to coordinate your every need; be it food drops, paying the bills, answering your phone calls, praying for your safe keeping, or dealing with the many disruptions that can occur over a six-month period.

The second echelon of support falls to the many benevolent people who reside in the small towns located near the AT. They were the one's who offered transportation, lodging, food, water, fuel, and encouragement when you most desperately needed it. They became known as "trail angels," as they always seemed to be watching out for others. A special thanks to Earl and Margie Towne of Andover, Maine; they represent the highest order of altruism in their mission to serve those who come their way.

Thirdly, it would be impossible to traverse this vast wilderness trail without the hard working, dedicated maintenance volunteers. They are the one's responsible for keeping the footpath clear of obstacles, re-routing trails, building and upgrading shelters, preserving the ecological balance, and a multitude of other services.

The final tier to this supporting cast would be the fellow hikers. They were there to share your burdens, hurt when you hurt, offer encouragement when you want to quit, share food and water with you when they are low on rations, and offer up a sense of humor to make you laugh when you want to cry.

In my case, my wife, Josephine, may as well have followed me and helped carry my pack. Her burdens at home far outweighed my 53 lb. pack, as she carried all of the aforementioned responsibilities of the home front, not to mention the concern over our son's health. It was she who encouraged me to stay on the trail, when in my heart, I knew that she needed me at home. So, to Josephine, I grant you the full recognition of having hiked the 2,160.4 miles from Georgia to Maine. Without you and all of the others, I could never have made it. Indeed, it took a village.

A special thanks to my son, Chris, a computer genius, who bailed me out at every turn. Without his technical assistance, this book would never have made it to print. Thanks to Kate Clabough for her editorial advice, consultation, and design of the trail map.

INTRODUCTION

Although I had talked of hiking the Appalachian Trail (AT) from Georgia to Maine for many years, it was not until I reached my 60th birthday that I decided that the time was right to set out on this great adventure. The summer of 1996 found me scurrying about the local outfitters checking out the various types of gear that I would need for the trek. There seemed to be a wealth of publications available and I read them all to acquaint myself with the trail experiences of other long distance hikers. In every respect, I was nothing more than a novice hiker. While I had hiked several trails in the Great Smoky Mountain National Park (GSMNP), it was not until February of 1997 that I experienced my first overnight outing in 20 years. This excursion took place primarily so that I could test some of my equipment.

In retrospect, I was certainly not the avid outdoors person that would have a variety of first hand experiences to draw from in order to take on the challenge of hiking some 2,000 miles. The day that I had planned so diligently for finally arrived. In the early hours of the 10th day of March 1997, my wife, Josephine, and I departed for Amicalola Falls State Park, near Ellijay, Georgia. The trip encompassed 175 miles and took us on back roads that we had never traveled. The weather was overcast and left one with a foreboding feeling that invoked mixed emotions of both, excitement and apprehension.

We arrived at the Visitor's Center around mid-morning, signed the trail log, weighed my pack (56 lb. without water), and then followed the road map to USFS Road 42. This was the most popular jumping off spot for those thru-hikers that chose not to tackle the 8.1 approach trail that led from the Visitor's Center to the top of Amicalola Falls. This very steep ascent to the top of the falls was not part of the official mileage for those who would reach the terminus in Maine.

It was 1145 when I bid a choked-up farewell to Josephine in the parking lot that led 0.9 miles to the top of Springer Mountain. I took solace knowing that I would see her again in approximately 16 days, providing that I was able to stay on schedule with my meticulously prepared itinerary. The family joke was that, I "would never get out of Georgia," let alone reach Fontana Dam, North Carolina. This very abbreviated accounting certainly does not encompass all that transpired prior to my journey, but should suffice to set the stage for what would become the greatest physical and mental challenge of my life.

Following completion of my journey, I spent the first ninety-days transcribing my journal notes. With the encouragement of others, I have decided to publish an accounting of my experiences. I have concluded that my daily struggles could possibly be helpful to prospective thru-hikers. Beyond this noble thought, I would hope that my journey would serve to enlighten, and perhaps, entertain anyone who might have the slightest interest in the great outdoors. My greatest desire is to provide the reader with an overall perspective of the joys and travails of such a journey.

The Appalachian Trail extends some 2,160 plus miles from Springer Mountain, Georgia to Mt. Katahdin, Maine. This great American footpath took me through 14 states, six national parks, eight national forests, and numerous mountain ranges; this distance can be broken down into five distinct regions:

Southern Mountains – GA, NC, TN (450 miles)

Virginia Highlands – VA (544 miles)

Mid-Atlantic Lowlands – WV, MD, PA, NJ, NY   (437 mile)

Southern New England – CT, MA (142 miles)

Northern New England – VT, NH, ME (588 miles)

While this is not intended to be a "how-to-book" for would-be long distance hikers, I will lay out three major components that kept me going. The **Physical**, the **Psychological**, and the **Spiritual**; each component will be become apparent to the reader as you follow my footsteps toward Mt. Katahdin, ME.

LET'S TALK EQUIPMENT

It makes little difference how much you spend for footwear, backpacks, sleeping bags, tents, water filters, etc. There are numerous books available touting the virtues of certain brand name trail essentials, and I read all that I could get my hands on prior to setting out on my journey. In fact, my initial obsession was tied directly to procuring the right equipment for the trail. Believe me, there is no such thing. If you grew up in a family that drove Chevrolets, you probably stuck with General Motors products. If your family voted Republican, you probably followed suit. The same holds true for hiking paraphernalia, so I won't bother you with my own biases.

I have listed my personal gear by brand, and price (Appendix A), simply to give readers a frame of reference should they decide to equip themselves for the trail. In no way is my equipment list to be passed off as "the right stuff;" that lies within each of us, and everyone has a unique ability to draw from this. Some are more successful than others, but we all have the capacity to achieve much more than we think we can.

GETTING A HANDLE

Most, if not all, long distance AT hikers encumber themselves with a trail name. Some choose a name that characterizes them, while a few simply amble up the trail, and wait for others to choose a name that fits them. I happened to be one of the compulsive one's who chose his own trail name, *Easy Strider*. This handle never quite fit and after 450 miles, I changed my trail name to *Reveille.*

I have elected to alter the trail names of the hikers that I met and traveled with on my journey to Maine. This is done out of respect for their privacy, although I suspect that none would object to having their real trail names divulged. On the other hand, I have depicted the people, other than hikers, in real world context. These people would include the keepers of hostels, motels, beds and breakfast, shops, day hikers, and good Samaritans, in general. For the most part, this later group can be described in glowing terms. My negative encounters with non-trail people could be counted on one hand.

THE PHYSICAL

On the 12th day of September, 1996 I reached my 60th birthday. I viewed this milestone as the proper time to retire from employment, and set out to realize my dream of hiking the 2,160.4-mile Appalachian Trail (AT) from Georgia to Maine. I had little difficulty in convincing myself that I deserved this opportunity; to say that my wife shared my outlook would be a stretch, better yet, a downright lie. I retired from the U.S. Army in September 1989, and had worked in the mental health field for another seven years. Both experiences helped me put together a certain mindset or determination to hike the entire AT.

So much for that, as I want to specifically address the physical aspects of preparing for my journey. My normal body weight generally ranged from 168 to 173 lbs. I was taking prescription medication for elevated cholesterol at the time of my departure. My only other physical limitation was due to a lawnmower accident in 1967. I had severed one-half of my great toe and the entire next appendage on my right foot while mowing a riverbank. I had never considered this to be disabling in any way. In fact, outside of my immediate family, no one would ever suspect that I had these missing appendages.

I purposely increased my body weight by at least 10 lb. I began loading my pack with 30 plus lb. and hiked all of the steep inclines near home. My favorite testing ground was the unfinished portion of the Foothills Parkway, adjacent to the Great Smokey Mountain National Park (GSMNP). I would hike 8-10 miles with my loaded pack mainly to break in my boots and toughen my feet. I gradually worked my pack weight up to 50 lb. with no major difficulty. I was only fooling myself though, as my test runs were usually on gradual inclines with no obstacles such as boulders, streams, or roots. Even to this day, I find it amusing that I considered myself to be in good shape for the trail. The bottom line is this; my physical conditioning took place during my first 16 days on the trail in the rugged mountains of northern Georgia and western North Carolina.

I weighed 179 lb. when I arrived at Amicalola Falls, the jumping off point in Georgia. By the time that I reached Fontana Dam, North Carolina, some 16 days later, I had lost 20 lb. This was not typical for most hikers. My body was reacting to the extreme physical demands placed on it, coupled with the fact that I could not keep food on my stomach for a good portion of the trek. My pack weight was entirely too heavy for my body structure even though I had taken great pains to carry only the essentials. It was amazing how my definition of "essential" would change as I moved northward. A pocketknife would give way to a penknife; pancake mix and syrup was out; and nesting pots gave way to a single titanium pot. I would eventually send my 20-degree sleeping bag home and make do with a sleeping bag liner. Before entering the "100-mile wilderness" in Maine, I would even send home my trusty water filter and make do with iodine tablets. As for my Whisper Lite stove, I never gave a moment's thought to sending it home.

There are a few realistic things that one can do to assure the ability to physically endure the hardships of the trail: (1) Get a physical, (2) Break in your hiking boots, and (3) Hike uneven terrain with a loaded pack (30-50 lb.). If you follow these three basics, you will figure out the rest on your own, as you make your way out of Georgia. Remember that your feet bear the brunt of the daily rigors of the trail. Don't leave out of Georgia or Maine with tender feet. You wouldn't begin a 2000-mile road trip in your vehicle on slick, worn tires; the same holds true for a successful journey on the AT.

THE PSYCHOLOGICAL
(MENTAL/EMOTIONAL)

Just how do you prepare yourself for the mental/emotional aspects of a 2000-mile hiking journey? The honest answer is, "You can't" ... that is, not entirely. My years in the mental health field had served to make me aware of the psychological aspects of stress brought on by physical hardships. Looking back, I now realize that my Army days, also served to provide me with a certain "can do" attitude. I would be remiss if I didn't confess a certain amount of do-or-die stubbornness handed down through my mother's side of the family. I had also developed an appreciation for poetry, especially that which extolled the virtues of perseverance, fortitude, and the like. I found myself clipping motivational pieces and committing some to memory. I was infatuated with the works of Robert W. Service who had roamed the Yukon Territories during the Gold Rush era of the early 1900's. In fact, when I was stationed at Fort Greely, Alaska in the mid – 1970's, I had committed to memory three of his most famous ballads: *The Shooting of Dan McGrew*, *The Cremation of Sam McGee*, and *The Spell of the Yukon*. I armed myself with these three ballads, and little did I realize just how important they would become to me as I plodded my way northward to Maine.

In addition, I used the doubting statements of my family and others pertaining to my ability to withstand the hardships of the trail. On more than one occasion, my family would jokingly state, "You'll never get out of Georgia." When I reached Fontana Dam some 16.5 days after departing Amicalola Falls, I would never hear doubts expressed by my family. There were others who did not openly state their reservations to me; one such family friend exclaimed to my wife, "Just let him talk about it, you know he's not going to do it." I filed these doubting sentiments away in my psyche and pulled them up every single time that I felt like giving in to the trail.

On a more personal and sensitive note, our son's illness gave me great inspiration. Chris had undergone a lower bowel resection due to ulcerative colitis two months prior to my start on the AT. On Day 49 of my journey, I was summoned off the trail as Chris had suffered a blockage and was scheduled for emergency surgery. This would be his third surgical procedure in five months. During this entire ordeal, Chris remained positive, and very sparingly used the morphine drip that was available to ease his pain. Not once did he complain to the nursing staff, and by all standards, he was a model patient. The mere thoughts of his "involuntary" suffering versus my "voluntary" suffering would often move me to tears.

I remained off the trail for eight days until Chris was ready for discharge. I suppose that my obsession to complete the AT in one season overrode sound judgment. Josephine was beginning to wear under multiple stressors, excluding Chris' medical ordeal. If there was ever a time that I should have come off the trail, it was at this juncture.

THE SPIRITUAL

I purchased the bulk of my hiking gear from Little River Trading Company in Maryville, Tennessee. Their business card contained the inscription, *"I can do all things through Christ who strengthens me," Philippians 4:13.* I suppose that this business card helped me focus on the importance of one's spiritual life when facing life's challenges. During a Sunday morning service at First Baptist Seymour, the choir director led an old standard hymn entitled, *"Victory in Jesus."* In fact, the first congregational response was so humdrum that the director called for a second response. The second time around, the congregation responded in a manner that would have delighted the composer of this hymn. The tempo was so uplifting, that I kept the church bulletin that had the words to this old gospel hymn in bold print. This hymn would become my anthem as I trudged my way northward towards Mount Katahdin in Baxter State Park, Maine. The small, pocket-sized, New Testament found a place in the upper compartment of my pack, along side my *Appalachian Trail Data Book*. I didn't realize it at first, but the verses contained in *I Corinthians, Chapter 13*, would come alive through the many compassionate and caring people that I would encounter, both on and off the trail.

Being of the Baptist faith, the need to witness to others is expected; quite honestly, I had never been very good at this. I suppose that I, like many other Christians, feared the prospects of rejection when sharing our faith. Whatever the case, it was not long before I began to share my faith with a few hiking partners, as we climbed out of Northern Georgia. I found that few would challenge the concept of a higher power, but fewer yet, would acknowledge their strong belief in a deity. I was becoming more timid in expressing my faith and didn't feel good about this. It would take some time and 450 miles of the trail before I would "plant my feet on higher ground," and openly express my faith. I maintained contact with my Sunday school class, and felt their presence as they lifted up my well being in their prayers.

While there is a vast difference between "voluntary" vs. "involuntary" hardships, the daily struggles of a thru-hiker forces one to deal with adversity with greater introspection. If you will, it is sort of like a self-imposed "traumatic stress disorder." Early in my journey, I considered good fortune events to be attributable to luck. I would later discover and recognize the presence of something far greater, as I made my way northward to Maine. My final entry in the trail register at Daicey Pond Lean-to in Baxter State Park, read ... *"Don't forget to thank your Higher Power, whatever that might be, for the kindness of strangers, and safe passage throughout this very long journey."*

-1-
CLIMBING OUT
GEORGIA

DAY 1 – March 10, 1997

By noon, the sky was becoming increasingly overcast, and it was chilly enough for me to don my insulated rain gear. As I took my first steps upward to the summit of Amicalola Falls, I nervously surveyed the trail for signs of the 2"x 6" white blazes that would ultimately guide me through 14 states on my journey to Mt. Katahdin, Maine. Upon reaching the summit, I took a picture of the bronze plaque imbedded in a rock near the falls. I hurried my pace, as I wanted to reach my first day's objective, Hawk Mountain Shelter, before sunset. I soon found myself back at the parking lot where I had left Josephine only a short time ago. I wished that I had paid more attention to the trail map, as I might have seen her once again. I had walked the first 1.8 miles of the AT, only to cross the same parking lot on my way to Hawk Mountain Shelter. Oh well, I hoped that this would not be an omen of things to come, as I never claimed to possess a good sense of direction.

It wasn't long before I met another north-bounder, a young man from Georgia, who was hobbled by two bad knees. His trail name was *Wise One,* and he was out to test his knees after his doctor had told him that he would probably never be able to do strenuous climbs. His goal was to walk as far as his knees would carry him. As we continued towards the shelter, I noticed that the trail was anything but smooth. Little did I know that the grapefruit-sized rocks would seem like mere pebbles in comparison to those that I would encounter in the months ahead.

When we reached the shelter at Hawk Mountain, it was almost packed out, but *Wise One* and I were able to squeeze in on the bottom deck. You could sense that social groups had already formed, and the more experienced hikers spoke of the tough climbs that were yet to come. Blood Mountain seemed to be the main topic of conversation. The bond fire felt good and cast an aroma that made one appreciate the great outdoors. A section hiker's dog bummed food and licked all of the empty containers. As much as I liked dogs, I began to sense that animals in a packed shelter were more of a nuisance that I would want to tolerate.

As the day concluded, U.S. Army helicopters buzzed the area several times. Army Ranger training was carried out in much of the mountainous area near Dahlonega, and night exercises took place all through the evening hours. *Wise*

One and I hit the sack early, as we planned to get an early start the next day. So much for sleep ... a hiker from New Jersey, by the name of *Shaman,* snored so loudly that most of the shelter occupants left their perches to seek comfort on the ground away from the shelter. I was able to withstand the onslaught by listening to my radio headset in order to drown out the incessant reverberations of this world-class snorer. (mile 7.7)

DAY 2 – March 11, 1997
Wise One and I departed Hawk Mountain at 0800. Originally, we had planned to stay at Gooch Gap Shelter, but decided that we did not want to endure another night of *Shaman's* snoring. At day's end, we had walked nine miles and set up camp on top of a mountain overlooking Suches, GA. *Quite Spirit* caught up with us and decided to join us for the night. As the night was very cold, Wise *One* attempted to build a campfire; he gave up on the idea after the wind blew embers all about the camp. *Quiet Spirit* offered tips on operating our camp stoves, and we turned in early after a hot meal. (mile 16.7)

<u>Author's Note</u>: **My 20-year military career left me with the engrained habit of expressing time according to the twenty-four-hour system. The P.M. hours may be difficult at first, but you will figure them out as you go. It is quite simple if you merely add the no. 12 to each hour beginning at 1:00 P.M. (1300), 2:00 (1400), 3:00 (1500), etc. Mid-night is expressed as 2400.**

DAY 3 – March 12, 1997
Wise One and I left with *Quiet Spirit*, a disable Vietnam veteran, who spent much of his spare time walking sections of the AT. He proved to be of great assistance to us novice hikers, and readily offered advice and assistance in a constructive manner. When we reached Woody Gap, *Wise One* decided to call it quits as his knees were really bothering him.

We took a break at a road crossing, bid farewell to our friend, and forged ahead towards the much-dreaded Blood Mountain; this would be Georgia's highest peak on the AT, at 4,461 feet. According to legend, this mountain was the site of a fierce battle between the Creek and Cherokee nations. The aftermath left so many dead and wounded that the slopes ran red with blood. This would be the first of many difficult climbs. Several hikers were milling about the summit when we arrived. The shelter atop Blood Mountain was made of stone and had been constructed by members of the Civilian Conservation Corps in the 1930's. I took one look inside the shelter and knew in a heartbeat that I would not be staying there. Dampness and filth permeated the structure, and there was little doubt that rodents had their way with anyone who might dare spend the

2

night in their domain.

Following some photos, *Quiet Spirit* and I made our way to Neels Gap, where we hoped to garner a bunk space at Walasiyi Center. Much to our disappointment, all bunks had been taken at the hostel, but we were able to shower and do a washing. It was here that I was introduced to my first pint of Ben and Jerry's ice cream, Chunky Monkey. I knew that this would be the first of many pints that I would consume along the way. We caught a ride to a nearby roadside park and camped for the night. (mile 30.8)

DAY 4 – March 13, 1997

I left Walasiyi Center at 1045. *Quiet Spirit* stayed behind to await a new Mountain Smith pack that was being sent directly from the manufacturer in CO. The climb out of Neels Gap was very steep and by mid-afternoon, the weather had begun to turn foul. The wind was brisk and what began as light rain eventually turned to sleet. A bird followed me along the trail as if to beg for food. I tossed a bit of gorp on the trail and hastened my steps in pursuit of the next shelter. By now the leaves on the trail were saturated with rain and sleet, and today, I took my first hard spill. Fortunately, I fell in such a manner that my pack absorbed most of the impact.

Soon after, I meet two female thru-hikers by the names of *Ginger* and *Nutmeg*. We walked together for a few miles, and then I went ahead while *Nutmeg* waited for her partner to catch up. Due to the bad weather, I cut my day short and moved towards Whitley Gap Shelter. I didn't relish the idea of walking 1.4 miles off the AT in order to reach this shelter. I would have moved ahead, if hypothermia had not been a concern.

When I arrived at the shelter, a section hiker by the name of *Brian* had already bedded down. *Ginger* and *Nutmeg* arrived about 30 minutes behind me. We immediately crawled into our sleeping bags in an effort to get warm. I was too sick to cook and snacked on whatever I could manage to keep down. The two women cooked Mac & Cheese and the mere thought of eating that goo made me even more nauseous. My Walkman radio really came in handy; I found a good gospel station and sacked out. (mile 37.1)

DAY 5 – March 14, 1997

The rain and wind continued throughout the night. *Ginger* and *Nutmeg* left before 0800. I decided to linger awhile longer in hopes that the rain would subside. Finally, I departed around 0930 and the steady rain didn't make the 1.4-mile climb out of Whitley Gap any easier. It rained for the next 6.5 miles and I was drenched to the bone when I finally arrived at Low Gap Shelter.

I arrived just in time to claim the next to last shelter space; we were packed in like sardines. I immediately changed out of my wet clothing and hastily cooked some chocolate pudding that sufficed as my evening meal. I was becoming concerned about my loss of appetite, but the thought of solid food made me even more nauseous. If these last two days of rain and cold don't turn me around, nothing will. This was the first time that I realized just how much I detested staying in shelters, and I vowed to tent as often as possible. Again, I was thankful for my radio, and all of the good reception in these mountains of northern Georgia. (mile 43.6)

DAY 6 – March 15, 1997

I spent a miserable night at Low Gap Shelter; the temperature plummeted to 25 degrees, not including the wind chill factor. My boots were frozen stiff, and my water bladder hose was completely iced over. I left the shelter at 0800 and met up with *Thistle-Burr,* who hailed from Indiana. He was about my age and had recently retired from his factory job. His hometown newspaper had highlighted his aspirations for completing the AT in one season, and he was feeling the pressure to succeed. Today, I seemed to feel a little better; could be that my body is becoming acclimated to the rigors of the trail. *Thistle-Burr* and I ate breakfast at mid-morning and pushed on to a campsite 0.5 short of Blue Mountain Shelter.

We set up camp around 1330 and dried some of our equipment. *Ginger* and *Nutmeg* came in by mid-afternoon and set up near us. My guess was that they felt safe with two old codgers old enough to be their fathers. I planned to leg it out tomorrow. *Thistle-Burr* planned to leave the trail at Hiawassee, GA for a couple of days in order to visit a relative. During the night the temperature dropped to 20 degrees, and our water bottles were frozen solid. *Thistle-Burr* had placed his dentures in a flask of water and you can guess what happened next. It was here that I first experienced the night sounds of the great horned owl. The cold, crisp air lent further splendor to their bold hoots that pierced the evening skies. There was little doubt that the horned owls owned the night forest, and all rodents had best be tucked safely in their domain. (mile 48.1)

DAY 7 – March 16, 1997

We broke camp at 0730 heading for a 12.7-mile trek across some of Georgia's roughest terrain. We walked straight up for 3-4 miles at a time; this section was known to weed out the faint of heart. I bypassed Tray Mountain Shelter and tented near Sassafras Gap, while *Thistle-Burr* decided to hold up at the shelter.

4

At day's end, Ginger, Nutmeg, and Carrot Top, who tented nearby, joined me. The difficult climbs really took their toll and I crashed early. The thoughts of more steep terrain weighed heavily on my mind, as I planned my next day's climb to Plumb Orchard Gap Shelter. (mile 59.4)

DAY 8 – March 17, 1997

I broke camp before the women and headed for the next shelter; the 13.1 miles traversed no less than five gaps. This simply stated, meant that you climbed and descended five separate ranges in order to reach Plumb Orchard Gap Shelter. When I arrived at the shelter, *Gizzard*, a Harley biker from Canton, OH, and *Whisper*, a 19 year-old lad from Lexington, KY, were already settled in at the shelter. *Carrot Top* came in shortly after my arrival and we spread out in this spacious shelter.

This was the Crown Jewel of Georgia's shelters; it had three levels, to include a pitched sleeping loft. I gave *Whisper* the pancake mix that I had been lugging through the mountains for naught, and he was only too happy to reduce my pack weight. In return, he showed me how to pull maintenance on my Whisper Lite stove, and I boiled extra water for shaving. I believe that this was my second time to shave, the first being at Walasi-yi Center at Neels Gap. Today, I made a decision to shave my mustache for the first time in over 20 years. I wasn't about to grow a beard and the mustache was becoming unmanageable, so it had to go. I crashed at 1900. (mile 72.5)

DAY 9 – March 18,1997

I was awake at 0600, had coffee and grits, did my moleskin thing, and took my time packing up. I left Plumb Orchard Gap Shelter at 0930 on the last leg of Georgia's AT. I arrived at the GA/NC line at exactly 1153; was I ever relieved to put the mountains of northern Georgia behind me. I had planned to celebrate this event by smoking the cigar that I had carried over the past nine days, but my stomach couldn't tolerate the thought of cigar smoke. Instead, I celebrated my accomplishment by reveling in the fact that I had "climbed out of Georgia," a fete that my family did not believe that I could accomplish. My exuberance for having made it through the rugged Georgia terrain was short-lived, as I could not tell any difference in the steep ridges of North Carolina. I was still walking uphill in the rain and didn't bother to stop to take a picture of the boundary sign separating the two states.

I arrived at Muskrat Creek Shelter at 1450. Three day-hikers followed me in, and I immediately fired my stove and drank some chicken broth. I felt sick afterwards, but managed to eat some chocolate pudding. Around 1700, four

5

other hikers showed up. By this time, the shelter was packed out and at least two hikers found semi-dry spaces under the shelter floor. I'm confident that they shared space with the mice, as did the rest of us who crammed into the limited floor space directly above. The weather report called for rain throughout the night with more of the same for tomorrow. I'll probable end up at Carter Gap Shelter tomorrow night. (mile 78.6)

At this juncture, it really hadn't dawned on me that my body was recoiling from the stress of the trail. I had no appetite for solid food, and vomited much of what I did eat. I had filtered every drop of water that I had consumed, thus reducing the prospects that I had contracted *Giardia*. None of my fellow hikers seemed to be experiencing my symptoms. I knew one thing for sure ... I was hurting, for whatever reason. I didn't realize it now, but I was only one day away from fighting the agonizing thoughts of coming off the trail.

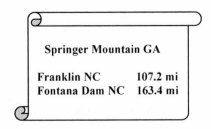

Springer Mountain GA

| Franklin NC | 107.2 mi |
| Fontana Dam NC | 163.4 mi |

-2-
SICK AS A DOG
NORTH CAROLINA

DAY 10 – March 19, 1997
It rained all night and even harder just before daylight. The three day-hikers and their dog left around 0830, and the people under the shelter welcomed their floor space. I ate a hot pack of Jell-O and planned to eat some oatmeal later. I may hold up here until the storm front moves through. I am becoming anxious to reach Rainbow Springs Campground in hopes of drying out, and eating some store-bought food.

I left the shelter with *Music Man*. He and I hit it off well due to our interest in music and sports. We walked in a soaking rain all the way to Standing Indian Shelter, only to find that the shelter was completely full. The three day-hikers had floor space, and you could tell that they felt sorry for all of the thru-hikers who were denied shelter space.

Soon after our arrival, the three day hikers decided to move on to Carter Gap Shelter, some 7.5 miles away. I decided to go with them even though this would push my day beyond 12 miles. They shared some of their venison jerky with me and it seemed to give me strength to move ahead. By now, the trail was running full of water and it seemed as though we were walking in a streambed. The three walked faster than I, and were soon out of sight. For the very first time since leaving Springer Mountain, I began to question why I would want to tolerate such hardship when I could be at home eating hot, delicious food and sleeping between sheets in the comfort of my home. I tried hard to dismiss these thoughts, but they stayed with me throughout this dreadful day.

I don't know what time I arrived at Carter Gap Shelter, as I was hurting so badly, and the dark, damp, overcast surroundings seemed to obliterate my sense of timing. Fortunately, there was floor space for me and the five other hikers. I was able to eat a 3-oz. can of tuna and some crackers. It was small wonder that I was loosing weight so rapidly. Although I didn't realize it at the time, I was merely lugging my food along the trail while other hikers were consuming at least two pounds of food each day. They were reducing their pack weight considerably, not to mention the much needed calories that they were consuming. The weather is supposed to clear tomorrow. (mile 91.2)

DAY 11 – March 20, 1997

I was the last person to depart Carter Gap Shelter on this, the first day of spring. The mid-morning sun felt good after two solid days of miserable rain. The three section hikers, *Whisper*, and *Uno* were ahead of me; this was the first time that I had been alone on the trail. I climbed Albert Mountain, the steepest short climb, yet; it was only a half-mile, but seemed much longer.

Today, I walked a little over 10 miles and camped on a hill overlooking Franklin, NC. I forced down some potatoes and gravy and turned in for the night. I seemed excited that I had only a short 3.5 miles tomorrow before reaching Rainbow Springs Campground. I really need a shower, not to mention some store-bought food. Hey, I hit the 100-mile mark today! (mile 101.2)

DAY 12 – March 21, 1997

Just the stars and me last night. I awakened to a beautiful sunrise and the promise of a high of 76 degrees for the afternoon. I departed camp around 0730, as I was anxious to reach Rainbow Springs Campground. In my haste, I missed a double white blaze at Wallace Gap.

I walked at least five miles out of the way before I met some locals who informed me that I was heading back towards Georgia ... was I ever disgusted with myself! This would not be the last dumb mistake that I would make. I reached RBS Campground before 1000. The camp store, owned by Buddy and Jessine Crossman, was a welcome site. I drank a pint of whole milk, as my stomach was still too uneasy to consume solid foods.

I rented a fish camp style cabin that seemed like a palace to me at this juncture. While the cabin was spartan by all measures, it afforded me a hot shower, a kitchen with a gas range, refrigerator, and a front porch with rockers overlooking the Nantahala River. A day of complete rest was just what I needed. *Music Man* came in shortly after me and also rented a cabin. I had hot dogs with chili and that was a big mistake, as I could not keep that down. I did manage to retain the cookies, milk, and ice cream that I consumed just before bedtime.

Before turning in for the night I lay on the sagging double bed, and smiled as I looked about the room ... if only Josephine could see me now. Tonight, I went to sleep listening to an old Motorola AM radio that picked up only three stations ... just like the 1950's. I loved it though! (mile 104.7)

DAY 12 – Cabin at Rainbow Springs Campground, Franklin, NC.

DAY 13 – March 22, 1997

    I was up early today and had eggs and pancakes. I couldn't eat all of the pancakes and gave the remaining to *Uno* who occupied the cabin next to mine. While I was checking out of the cabin, *Quite Spirit* came in to report that *Thistle-Burr* had fallen and broken his leg just before Albert Mountain.

    The Crossman's called 911, and the local MET crew came to the campground to get directions to where *Quiet Spirit* had left him on the trail. Fortunately, the MET crew had little difficulty in reaching him as he had left him on an accessible Forest Service Road. The soldier from *Quiet Spirit's* RVN tours came into play and you could tell that he was on a mission when he came into RBS Campground to report *Thistle-Burr's* misfortune.

    Music Man and I left RBS at 0915, and after walking about 10 miles, we spotted two young lads setting on the trail. *Music Man* was about to ask them about the trail up ahead when much to his surprise, he discovered that one of the lads was his son. They had intended to surprise him, and that, they did. We camped on a grassy bald, and the wind chill dropped the temperature to below freezing before nightfall. I was too sick to cook, and vomited most of the snack food that I had managed to consume. Around 0215, I gained the courage to get out of my sleeping bag and put on my polar tech underwear. The remaining early morning hours were marked by fitful sleep. (mile 114.7)

DAY 14 – March 23, 1997

I broke camp ahead of *Music Man* and headed for Wayah Bald Tower. Since this was Palm Sunday, I read from Matthew regarding Jesus' entrance to Jerusalem prior to his crucifixion. The views from the tower were impressive, and for the first time, I could see the Smoky Mountains.

Music Man caught up with me at the tower. We walked a little over 10 miles and met lots of weekend hikers along the way. The steep climbs were numerous, and we walked until 1700 before pitching our tents on some very uneven terrain near a spring. Once again, I vomited my evening meal. I didn't sleep well, but managed to stay comfortable in my tent, as the temperature dropped to near freezing. (mile 125.0)

DAY 15 – March 24, 1997

We broke camp by 0715. We were heading a short 10 miles to Wesser, NC and the Nantahala Outdoor Center (NOC), where we hoped to find lodging and some good restaurant food. We arrived at NOC around 1230. The steep descent to the Center really jammed my toes. Fortunately, I had placed moleskin in all the right places, thus sparing myself the agony of more blisters.

Much to our disappointment, college students on Spring break had occupied all of the NOC bunk spaces. We learned of a rental condo and called the owner who agreed to pick us up at the NOC. Our earlier disappointment quickly dissipated, as we soon found ourselves in the restaurant consuming cheeseburgers, fries, and about a gallon of the best iced tea that I had ever drunk. I ordered a carryout BLT, with Texas fries, and homemade apple pie. The owner came for us and we were driven 3.5 miles to a spacious condo with two double beds, a bath, and plenty of hot water. You can't begin to comprehend the value of hot water after being exposed to the elements for days at a time. Crawling in between sheets this night seemed too good to be true. (mile 134.4)

DAY 16 – March 25, 1997

We thumbed a ride to NOC with a young lady who worked there. The 3.5-mile ride in the back of her pickup was a little bit on the chilly side, but we didn't complain. We downed a double stack pancake breakfast with sausage patties, and 5-6 cups of coffee. We ate as if this would be our last meal. I couldn't eat all of my pancakes and took one of the sausage patties with me for the trail.

We departed NOC around 0930 and began the dreaded climb up the mighty Cheoah mountain range. I could hardly wait to climb this section of the AT, as everyone had been talking about the ruggedness of the terrain. It was just as difficult as everyone had indicated, and fortunately for me, this was the best that I had felt since departing Springer Mountain, two weeks ago. I separated from *Music Man*, who walked with *Carrot Top*, *Ginger* and *Nutmeg*.

We all ended up at Locust Cove Gap, 10.5 miles beyond the NOC. My appetite has picked up, and I ate three hot items and a cup of banana pudding. The camping area left much to be desired and, as we bedded down, the small area was filled with six tents. I turned in at 1830 and listened to my radio until dark. I hope to get and early start in the morning ... good chance for rain tonight. (mile 144.9)

DAY 17 – March 26, 1997

The rain came just before midnight and poured throughout the early morning hours; I managed to stay dry even with some seepage around the bottom of my tent. *Music Man* had to wake me this morning ... that's a change ... I'm usually the first one to rise. I crammed my wet tent into a large plastic bag and we set out for the next major climb; come to think of it, that's all we ever do!

When we came off the Cheoah's at Stecoah Gap, we hung our wet gear on a rail fence that bordered a pull-off with two picnic tables. The trail ahead was the toughest climb thus far; the Stecoah Mountain range seemed to never end. Water was plentiful and the blue skies seemed to take away the pain of the never-ending climbs. Just when you began to believe that you must be ready for a downhill descent, there would be another switchback; that could mean only one thing ... another steep climb. This was a section that had turned many a hiker back to the comforts of home.

When we reached Yellow Creek Mountain Road, we took a much-deserved 20-minute pack-off break on a grassy knoll. We were now only 0.9 of a mile from our destination, Cable Gap Shelter. We passed up the final two floor spaces in the shelter in lieu of tenting. A creek ran beside the tent area and the moisture seemed to add to the cold night air that we had become so accustomed to. We did have a privy and that was a welcome luxury. I cooked a rice dinner, filtered my water for the next day, and turned in at 1800. Atlas, I seemed to be over my vomiting episodes and my appetite is much improved. I am excited about tomorrow and the prospects of reaching Fontana Dam. (mile 156.6)

DAY 18 – March 27, 1997

I was so excited about reaching Fontana Dam that I awoke every 2-4 hours; I was packed and ready to travel by 0700. Fontana Lake was a beautiful site with the early morning fog lifting off the reservoir. I took several pictures as the sun beamed down on a crisp morning that found us making our way down the long, winding trail leading to the Visitor's Center at Fontana Dam. We could see the dam for miles before we arrived, at 1045.

I called Josephine, took my fourth shower in 18 days, shaved, and awaited her arrival. A gentleman and his grandson were kind enough to give me a cup of orange juice, as the concession stand inside the Visitor's Center was still closed for the season. As it turned out, the gentleman was the father of Warren Doyle, a trail guru, who had thru-hiked the AT more than a dozen times. *Music Man* planned to meet a friend and was picked up at noon for transport to a motel and restaurant. He planned to take a couple days off the trail, and we agreed to link up again following my Easter weekend visit with my family. We were the lead pack coming into the Dam, and I hoped that our trail buddies would come in before I depart, as Josephine plans to bring plenty of KFC and sodas. I had informed all that we would be treated to some real "trail magic" upon arrival at the dam.

I found a nice grassy area in a cul-de-sac above the dam and reclined on the grass in order to soak up the noonday sun. What a beautiful day … blue skies with very little cloud activity and a temperature of 82 degrees. It doesn't get any better than this! Josephine delivered as promised … KFC, sodas, apples, and brownies were waiting when my hiking buddies arrived; they were immensely grateful, and Josephine could only watch in utter amazement as we gorged ourselves. What a beautiful sunny day; God had truly blessed us all. (mile 163.4)

As I looked back on my climb out of the mountains of Northern Georgia and Western North Carolina, I could not help feeling gratified knowing that I had navigated one of the most rugged stretches of terrain that the Appalachian Trail had to offer. Despite the few days of miserable rain and cold, there was much to be thankful for in terms of the weather. The Farmer's Almanac had been on target predicting milder than normal temperatures for the month of March; I was glad that I had chosen the window of March 10th to begin my 2,000-mile journey to Mt. Katahdin, ME. In retrospect, my pack weight was well beyond the norm, and my early-on difficulty with keeping food on my stomach made the journey even more difficult. If there was any saving grace in the aforementioned, I suppose that my body hardened to the rigors of the trail more rapidly than most hikers. By the time that I reached Fontana Dam, NC, some 16.5 days after departing Springer Mountain, I felt confident that I had my "trail legs" fully beneath me!

Fontana Dam	
Birch Springs Shelter	5.5 mi
Newfound Gap	39.5 mi
Davenport Gap	70.4 mi

DAY'S 19/20/21 – March 28-30, 1997

I spent four nights and three days at home with my wonderful family. Following Easter Sunrise and church services, we ate lunch on the gazebo ... what great food! I have lost 20 pounds over the past 17 days and my cholesterol medication seems to be interfering with my metabolism. What a great time with the family. Josephine will meet me again at Newfound Gap on April 4th for resupply.

Music Man called to inform me that he was back on the trail, and we made plans to meet again at Hot Springs, NC. The hot soak baths, great food, and the company of my family will be hard to leave, but my determination to complete the entire 2,000 mile of the AT is stronger than ever. Even at that, I'll depart with mixed emotions when Josephine drops me off at Fontana Dam on March 31st.

FAMILY – son, Chris, and wife, Dawn, Josephine, and son, Mark.

-3-
TREKKING THROUGH THE SMOKIES
GSMNP

DAY 22 – March 31, 1997
    I left Josephine at Fontana Dam around 0930; she will meet me again at Newfound Gap on April 4th. The Great Smoky Mountain National Park holds 70.4 miles of the AT, and I planned to move through in seven days, weather permitting. As I was walking across the dam, I met a hiker by the name of *Wild Bill*, a retired New Jersey policeman, who had recently won several million dollars as his share of a lottery pool. He purchased his retirement plan, bid his fellow workers goodbye, and hit the trail. We were both headed for Birch Spring Shelter, and I went out ahead.

About two miles in, the skies clouded and it started spitting sleet. I donned my rain gear, as the wind chill quickly dropped to well below freezing. I arrived at the shelter, followed by *Digger* and *Wild Bill*. I ate some of the home cooked food that Josephine had prepared, and set about to make myself comfortable in a very dilapidated shelter. By 1400 the shelter was so cold that I had to resort to my cold weather gear. Three hikers from the United Kingdom, *Ox*, *Silver Fox*, and *Lizard* came in next, followed by *Morning Star*. I really liked the chatter of the Britt's, as they were always upbeat even though our environment was dismal. By nightfall, 12 hikers were crammed into the shelter, and most turned in early in an effort to keep warm. (mile 168.9)

DAY 22 - Birch Springs Shelter, GSMNP. The first of six shelters that I would spend the night during my 70.4-mile trek through the Smokies.

DAY 23 – April 1, 1997

I slept fairly well and awakened at 0500. I was on the trail by 0645, and looking forward to the weather forecast of a mild and sunny day. Ahead, I could see snowcaps on the distant slopes. I was thankful for my three-day break at home that allowed me to miss the recent snows through this section. The break had done wonders for my physical and mental well-being.

I had no difficulty in moving at a rapid pace to Spence Field Shelter. As usual, I was the first in, having arrived at 1230. A day-hiker came in and ate his lunch before heading back to Cades Cove. The hikers from last evening arrived by mid-afternoon. *No Doze* had joined up with the others, and he and *Morning Star* seemed to make a good twosome. For lunch, I had chicken soup with the pork chop that I had brought from home, topped off with coffee, and apple pie. These delicacies would be short-lived, and I would soon be back on the usual trail food. One thing for sure, my appetite has vastly improved, and I no longer have difficulty in keeping food on my stomach. Sleep did not come easy tonight; that *No-Doze* takes the prize, as a world-class snorer ... he never missed a beat! (mile 178.6)

DAY 24 – April 2, 1997

I was up at 0530 and on the trail by 0630. A herd of deer wandered about the shelter early this morning and they seemed to have no fear of us humans. Today, the weather was mild with virtually no wind. I climbed ole Rocky Top, and took pictures looking back towards Fontana Lake. I met two day-hikers as I crossed Thunderhead; I had skinned out of my polartech outing wear and was walking in shorts by mid-morning. At times the footing was precarious coming off Thunderhead due to snow and ice; so far, I've managed to keep my footing. I planned to stop at Derrick Knob Shelter to eat lunch. I encountered lots of tough, short climbs today.

I arrived at Siler's Bald Shelter at 1445. I met several hikers who were pushing through, so that they could get off in Gatlinburg for resupply. I'm lucky to have Josephine to resupply me at Newfound Gap, so that I can move through the GSMNP as quickly as possible. The shelters were unbelievably trashed by waves of school kids who were hiking through the Smokies while on the Spring break; not only this, but I detested having to stay caged up in the shelters due to bear activity. The shelter maxed out during the night with 13 hikers. (mile 190.4)

DAY 25 – April 3, 1997

I left Siler's Bald Shelter before 0630, heading towards my next overnight stay at Mt. Collins Shelter. The views back towards Fontana Lake were magnificent, and I took frequent breaks just to soak up the vastness of the mountain ranges. On the way, I met *Black Hawk,* who had worked on the Star Wars Project in Huntsville, AL. He had been laid off, and decided to hit the trail.

I arrived at Mt. Collins Shelter shortly after the noon hour. I wished that I had planned better, as I could have easily made it to Newfound Gap by 1500. My appetite is good and I am really looking forward to the food that Josephine will bring tomorrow. I was beginning to miss the group of hikers that had moved ahead of me during my time off over the Easter weekend. I was almost out of fuel today, and I was particularly surprised to find that a hiker had left a partially filled fuel bottle at Double Spring Gap shelter; what luck! Today, I met *Dave* and *Beth*, a Quaker couple, who elected to retain their given names in lieu of the traditional trail handles. I slept well knowing that I would see Josephine by noon tomorrow. (mile 198.4)

DAY 26 – April 4, 1997

What a gorgeous day; too bad the trail didn't reciprocate. The recent snows had begun to melt, leaving the trail a mushy quagmire. I passed Clingmans Dome, the highest peak on the AT, at 6,643 feet; overhead, some tourist peered down from the tower and inquired about our destination. I walked awhile with *Ink Spot*, a young wilderness counselor, from North Carolina. I arrived at Newfound Gap at 0910 and made my way to the restroom, where I shaved and took a quick spit bath. The mid-morning sun felt good, as I reclined against a retaining wall to await Josephine's arrival. Curious tourists would occasionally stop to ask questions about us thru-hikers; most were amazed that we were on our way to Maine ... to tell you the truth, I was somewhat amazed myself! One lady exclaimed with all seriousness, "Well, it should be all downhill from here."

I wished that I had asked Josephine to meet me before noon, as I was anxious to move ahead in order to catch up with *Music Man* and the others; they were at least two to three days ahead of me. While I was waiting, a day-hiker gave me a cherry coke and some snickers. Boy, did they ever taste good, and served as a warm up for all the goodies that Josephine would bring. She arrived at 1120, and would have been here earlier had she not gotten hung up in the Gatlinburg traffic. I was grateful that she was able to show up at all, as she felt so bad due to an ear infection. She brought the double whopper with cheese that I so desperately craved, along with fries and sodas ... not to mention chicken tenders, homemade cookies, and a quart of milk. What a feast!

When I departed, I felt like a pack mule, as my pack weight was near 60 lb. My energy level was peaked and I walked the 2.7 miles, straight up, to Ice Water Springs Shelter, in 1 hr. and 10 min. I was really smoking, so I decided to push on to Peck's Corner Shelter. I knew that it was going to rain, but didn't really care ... enough shelter life for me. With any luck, the shelter will be maxed out and I'll be on *terra firma* tonight. *Hans* and *Grettle*, a couple from Connecticut, and *No-Doze* tented beside me. *No-Doze* was at his best; he snored so loudly that the ground vibrated. (mile 213.3)

DAY 26 – Josephine met me at Newfound Gap, GSMNP, for resupply.

DAY 27 – April 5, 1997

The rains pelted most of the night, and I packed my wet gear in my plastic bag; I was beginning to really appreciate this huge, industrial strength bag. I had learned to top load all of my wet gear for easy retrieval; later in the day, I would string a line and let the wind and sun dry my gear.

The weather was threatening as I departed, but soon gave way to clear, blue skies with brisk winds; just what I needed to dry my gear. I kept my outing wear on until noon, and then walked in shorts and tee shirt for the remainder of the day. I enjoyed the great views of Pittman Center and Cosby Knob. I walked 13 miles today, and 15 miles yesterday. The last 2.6 miles in to Cosby Knob Shelter was very scenic. I stayed in the shelter, as I could not find a level area suitable for tenting; more rain in the forecast. I'll move on tomorrow to Mountain Mama's hostel where I hope to shower, wash some clothes, and partake of their much acclaimed cheeseburger. I set my watch ahead to DST, and turned in as the rain pelted the tin roof of the shelter. (mile 226.3)

DAY 28 – April 6, 1997

No-Doze and another hiker kept me awake most of the night with their incessant snoring ... that's it! I've made up my mind to bypass Mountain Mama's, and put some distance between these world-class snorers and me. I departed Cosby Knob Shelter at 0733 and walked in a steady drizzle for the next 7.5 miles. I made good time and arrived at Davenport Gap Shelter in slightly under 3 hours. I had just finished filtering some water when a heavy downpour kept me in the shelter for over an hour. I found some instant coffee and tea that had been left behind for "any thru-hiker," and boiled some water for a hot beverage. I hastened my steps towards the AT crossing at Interstate-40, as I was extremely anxious to put the Smokies behind me.

Someone had dismantled and defaced some of the AT signs and blazes where the trail crosses the Interstate; I had to rely on common sense to traverse this section of the trail. I felt a keen sense of relief, as I began a very steep climb towards Snowbird Mountain. I looked back at the fast moving Interstate traffic that was framed by the foliage of numerous white, flowering dogwoods. Spring was in the air and it felt good to be alive.

Water was plentiful and I hiked all day without seeing a single hiker. Most north bounders got off at Mountain Mama's for a cheeseburger. I had mine Friday, so I didn't feel deprived, as I forged ahead for a 15-mile walk before halting for the day. I camped on a sunny knoll short of Groundhog Creek Shelter. I'm amazed at how easy I am managing long mileage days; it has to be my food intake ... cccheeseeeburgers, cccccchickennnn fingers, ccccccookies, ... well, it took me long enough to reach this energy level. (mile 242.0)

My 70-mile trek through the Smokies was one that I vowed not to experience again. I had stayed in six of the 13 shelters along the AT; no more mandatory shelter life for me! In addition to being caged by wire fencing, the mice were ever-present and their droppings posed a Hantavirus threat. In addition, I had begun to realize that my early morning rising was not compatible with most hikers. Besides, I really coveted my privacy, and my two-person tent provided a perfect cocoon for my pack and me.

DAY 28 – Looking back, as I crossed Interstate-40. Spring was in the air and Hot Springs, NC was on my mind.

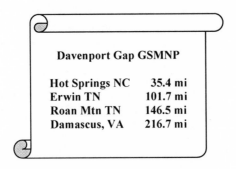

Davenport Gap GSMNP

Hot Springs NC	**35.4 mi**
Erwin TN	**101.7 mi**
Roan Mtn TN	**146.5 mi**
Damascus, VA	**216.7 mi**

ON THE TRAIL TO DAMASCUS
TENNESSEE/NORTH CAROLINA

DAY 29 – April 7, 1997
I left camp at 0740. The weather was clear, but very windy … I had to use my light windbreaker all day. The climbs were numerous and quite steep ... water was less plentiful, but sufficient. Max Patch summit was so windy that I was almost blown off my feet on occasions. This was my second day of walking without seeing a fellow human being.

I walked past Groundhog Creek Shelter and pushed on to Walnut Mountain Shelter, the oldest standing shelter on the AT, having been erected some 50 years ago. The shelter register revealed that *Music Man* had departed this shelter earlier today. As I prepared to spend the night alone, a German shepherd dog barked and startled me, as I was preparing my evening meal. A couple approached the shelter to claim their dog; they had been out for a day hike and I enjoyed their company. The lady took my home phone number and asked if it would be all right to call Josephine to let her know that they had talked with me. Of course, I gave my consent, but they never followed through. The evening was cool and crisp as I settled in for the night. (mile 257.0)

DAY 30 – April 8, 1997
I awakened alone to temperatures below freezing and departed Walnut Mountain Shelter at 0714. I made my way to Hot Springs without seeing a soul. I arrived at 1230 and checked in at the Duckett House Bed & Breakfast, a turn of the century farmhouse that was converted to a B&B in 1990. I had a private room with a shared bath and a great breakfast for $25.

After some shopping, I ran into *Music Man* and the original gang that I started with at Springer Mountain. It was good to see them again, and we made plans to depart the next day around mid-morning. I had restaurant food twice today, topped off with another pint of B&J ice cream. I enjoyed rambling about this little village that touts its hot mineral springs that earlier in the century had catered to wealthy tourists. Hot Springs has revived itself and once again offers a relaxing atmosphere for tourists and hikers who seek some respite here. I wrote letters to everyone on my list and felt my confidence surging. My appetite is great, and I seem to be getting stronger as I go. At this juncture, I'm about four days ahead of schedule. In looking at my trail log, I've managed to tent 50 percent of the time, and I have stayed in hostels on two occasions. (mile 269.8)

DAY 31 – April 9, 1997

I had a great breakfast at the Duckett House B&B, and we departed Hot Springs at 1000. It was a clear, crisp day, but that soon changed. The temperature dropped and the winds picked up, as we ascended Rich Mountain. Several thru-hikers left Hot Springs today; *Ginger* and *Nutmeg*, hereafter referred to as *The Spice Girls*, were among those departing. Atlas, I'm out ahead of *No-Doze*.

We arrived at Spring Mountain Shelter and tented on a hill overlooking the shelter. I counted seven tents and only five hikers sleeping in the shelter; could it be that I'm not the only one with an aversion to shelter life? *Quiet Spirit* gave me some much-needed advice on pack adjustment, as he also carried a Mountain Smith pack. I met *Sir Lancelot* for the first time today. He resides in Maine and is walking home. He's a tall, slim fellow who grew up in Great Britain and still has a trace of an English accent. We hit it off immediately, and he hiked with *Music Man* and me for the remainder of the day. (mile 280.7)

DAY 32 – April 10, 1997

As of today, we are two weeks out of Damascus, VA; so far, this group is hanging tough! We departed camp at 0810 and did 15.3 miles by 1700. As usual, lots of tough climbs today; we stopped at Little Laurel Shelter for lunch. Blackstack Cliffs was interesting and I took pictures of what I thought to be Shelton Laurel valley.

Music Man was slower today, as his blood pressure medication slows his heart rate on the steep climbs. I was pretty much bushed and had little difficulty turning in early. We made camp and planned for tomorrow's 14.6-mile trek to Hogback Shelter. *Music Man* has invited some of us to come off the trail at Erwin for an overnight stay with his sister and brother-in-law at in Kingsport. (mile 296.2)

DAY 33 – April 11, 1997

We walked the high ridges above Shelton Laurel; this area was of special interest to me as a result of my genealogy pursuit of my mother's ancestral ties to this area. I knew this to be "bushwhacker country," from Civil War days. I actually felt a foreboding sense, as I imagined what it might have been like for soldiers, from both sides of the conflict, who navigate this treacherous area. Literature reveals that the laurel thickets were so compacted that soldiers on horseback had to dismount and hack their way through the thick undergrowth.

The gigantic boulders strewn throughout the area most likely afforded the bushwhackers the cover they needed to ambush many an unsuspecting traveler. William R. Trotter's, *Bushwhackers, The Civil War in North Carolina,* and *Victims, A True Story of the Civil War,* by Phillip Shaw Paludan, capture the essence of this region.

I was anxious to reach the Shelton graves that lay next to the trail. Much to my delight, the gravesites were clearly visible from the trail, and *Music Man* took my picture at the site. I located the Shelton graves along side of two others; the inscriptions on the headstones read as follows: Wm. Shelton, Co E. 2N.C. INF and David Shelton, Co. C. 3N.C. MTD INF. While returning from their regiments for a visit with their families, the uncle and nephew had been ambushed by Confederate forces.

After soaking up a bit of history, we proceeded over the many huge boulders that made walking difficult at times. We crossed NC 212 at Devil Fork Gap and Boone Cove Road and walked a total of 14.6 miles to Hogback Shelter. I opted to pitch my tent even though rain was forecast for the night. *Music Man's* invitation for us to stay over at the home of his sister should be interesting; six grungy hikers with all of their gear, traveling to Kingsport. I wondered if his sister knew of her brother's generous hospitality. (mile 310.8)

DAY 34 – April 12, 1997

It rained most of the night. I decided to decline *Music Man's* gracious invitation. It was drizzling, as I jammed my rain soaked tent into my trusty plastic bag, and I was on the trail by 0745. *Speed Demon*, a young kid from Connecticut, passed me, but we met again at Sam's Gap, US 23.

By now the rain was steady, and we had both heard that there was a gas station within a mile of where the AT crossed US 23. We started walking, but found no gas station in sight. *Speed Demon* had an updated 1997 *Appalachian Trail Date Book* that indicated a restaurant was located three miles east of the trail. We continued our walk along the edge of this much traveled highway until we came to an old Esso station that had been converted to a restaurant.

Speed Demon wore earrings, and I suggested that he might consider removing them before we entered the establishment. Knowing the conservatism of this area and the anti-sentiment towards AT hikers, I felt that we would have a better chance of hitching a ride back to the trailhead. Neither of us relished the idea of the 4-5 mile climb back to where this chase had begun. He accepted my suggestion and we entered the restaurant under the gaze of locals who were having breakfast.

We took our seats at the counter and a none-to-friendly waitress took our orders. We had a great breakfast and *Speed Demon* ordered a second round. One of the waitresses spotted a trucker, and suggested that he might give us a ride back to the trailhead; he graciously nodded that he would, if we could be ready when he was. We assured him that we would be ready and we ordered sausage biscuits to go; we also purchased some praline squares that later proved to be great energy boosters.

We stowed our packs in the trailer of his 18-wheeler and jumped in the cab for the ride back to the AT. On the way, we spotted two more hikers chasing that "restaurant in the sky." We couldn't help but chuckle at our own ordeal in acquiring some much needed nourishment. *Speed Demon* went out ahead of me and, I soon met up with the *The Spice Girls*. As we climbed in a misty, dense fog, we met two locals harvesting ramps near a spring at the base of Big Bald. *The Spice Girls* were fascinated with this newly discovered "onion," and the locals gave them some to take with them. I pulled a few ramps to season my evening rice and bean dinner.

I forged ahead to Whistling Gap where I camped, and cooked my rice and beans with ramps ... boy, was it ever good. At day's end, I had walked 16.1 miles; that big breakfast and the praline candy did much towards this accomplishment. As I lay snuggled in my sleeping bag, I planned to do 13.8 miles tomorrow and be at Nolichucky Gorge Campground by mid-afternoon. (mile 326.9)

DAY 35 – April 13, 1997

The Spice Girls had camped near my tent site last evening, and during the night a hunting dog had prowled our camp. At first, I had no idea what was stirring about; when I got up to inspect the area, two glowing, green eyes startled me. I shouted, "Get out of here!" Later, I would learn that I had awakened the two women who were too afraid to get out of their tent to secure their equipment. We all got a chuckle out of the incident the next morning.

As I broke camp, it began to sprinkle rain ... lots of short climbs lay ahead. I met two ladies who were handing out chocolate chip cookies to us thru-hikers. Just before I reached the Nolichucky River, *Speed Demon* caught up with me, and we walked the last few miles together to the Nolichucky Expedition Campground, arriving at 1400.

We had begun to pitch our tents when we were approached by *Kampfire*, a nomadic sort, who had walked parts of the AT, and liked to assist thru-hikers with transportation to and from Erwin. He called Florida home, but I would later learn that he sort of drifted from Georgia to Maine providing services to us hikers. He lived in his conversion van, and relied on donations from hikers for services rendered. In the months to come, I came to know him as a genuinely caring individual who really enjoyed fellowshipping with us, as we struggled towards our destination in Maine. He offered *Speed Demon* and me a ride to Erwin for some much needed shopping. We immediately put our laundry on cycle and walked across the street to Little Caesar's Pizza, where we each purchased the largest pizza available; man, was I ever stuffed. *Kampfire* picked us up for the ride back to the campground where I sorted and packed my food and clothes.

In the distance, I heard train whistles and screeching brakes all through the night. I awakened at 2300 and couldn't go back to sleep. I went to the bathhouse and soaked my hands in some hot water ... it felt so good. Upon returning to my tent, I finished eating my raisin pie and drank more milk. I slept lightly for the remainder of the early morning hours. (mile 336.3)

DAY 36 – April 14, 1997
I was awake at 0530 and went to the bathhouse to soak my feet and hands in hot water. Next to restaurant food, hot water is about as good as it gets. I made plans to catch *Kampfire's* first shuttle back to Erwin at 0800. I went to the Post Office, grocery, and barbershop where I got my first "buzz job" since I was an 18-year old private. I thumbed a ride back to the campground with a Charles Erwin, a fine Christian man, who was headed for his church, but decided to take me all the way to my destination.

I departed the campground at 1245 and linked up with the *The Spice Girls* on the way to Beauty Spot Gap. Tent sites were hard to come by, and we reluctantly settled on a site close to a USFS Road. We always tried to avoid camping within sight of any back roads, but today had to be an exception. I haven't taken any of my cholesterol medication since leaving Fontana Dam. I am consuming as much fat as I can acquire, and that's not much. Most of our fats come from the food that we acquire when we get off the trail for resupply. If possible, I plan to get a cholesterol check at Damascus. The night sky was clear with stars clearly visible; it should be a great day tomorrow. (mile 146.0)

DAY 37 – April 15, 1997
Bone chilling cold this morning, and I didn't get out of my sleeping bag until 0630. I planned to hike 13.4 miles to Clyde Smith Shelter. Today, I met *Young-man* and *Sleepy*, two students from New Hampshire; they seem to be nice kids and I enjoyed their company. The British trio of *Ox*, *Silver Fox*, and *Lizard* are a day behind. Likewise, *Stumbling Al* is a day behind; I met him for the first time in Erwin ... seems to be a bit of a character. *Speed Demon* and *Insider* did a

30-mile "slack pack" out of Nolichucky; these guys were obsessed with speed.

This was my first encounter with the concept of "slacking." Basically, this is when a hiker walks without a pack. Someone takes the pack ahead to a planned rendezvous, thus affording the hiker the benefit of hiking without the pack weight. This was something that I vowed not to do. I wanted to follow the white blazes, and carry my full pack all of the way to my destination in Maine. I pitched my tent and was ready for bed around 2000. (mile 159.4)

DAY 38 – April 16, 1997

I left camp at 0739 and climbed for four hours. The weather was clear and I could see for great distances. I ate lunch at Roan High Knob Shelter, the highest shelter on the AT, at 6,285-feet. It was here that I met two ex-marines who were attending Georgia College; they gave me a quick lesson on the technique of tying a dew rag. Next came the long, steep climb at Carver's Gap. I met several groups of day hikers, and they all asked the obvious questions. "How long have you been hiking?" "Where did you start?" "How far are you going?" It was here that I began to affirm my response to the later question; no more, "I hope to, or plan to." It would forever after be, "I am going to Mt. Katahdin, Maine."

I made my way to Overmountain Shelter. This was a large, red barn that was featured in the film, *The Winter People*, starring Kurt Russell, Kelly McGillis, and Lloyd Bridges. I slept in the loft, and this would turn out to be my favorite shelter, and that was something, since I detested shelter life, in general. The thought of tenting near the barn never crossed my mind. *The Spice Girls*, *Young-man*, *Sleepy*, and *Jack* and *Jill* also stayed in the barn. Storm clouds had begun to form over the Humps by late afternoon, thus giving a clue as to what was in store for tomorrow's journey. I decided to move my sleeping pallet away from the loft door opening, and was I ever glad that I did. (mile 372.7)

DAY 39 – April 17, 1997

Just after midnight, the rain turned to sleet, and when we awoke this morning, I discovered that the barn loft near the door was covered with a light sprinkle of snow. Outside, the ground was covered and blankets of frozen fog shrouded the Humps. To add to this, the winds had picked up to the point that hypothermia became a concern. The other hikers were low on food, and *The Spice Girls* were completely out; I had given them a pasta dinner to help out last evening.

I watched the others depart around 0800, as the wind whipped fiercely at their parkas. I decided to wait out the ice fog and didn't leave the shelter until 1030. I prayed that all had made it safely to their destination at Elk Park where they would resupply. I had enough food to get me to the hostel near Hampton. I set out for the 13.8-mile trek to the Apple House Shelter and arrived at 1415. I planned to spend the night here, but decided to walk on to Hwy 19E where I hoped to find a restaurant. This final excursion of the day would turn out to be a most memorable one. I crossed a footbridge and made my way up a steep embankment to Hwy 19E, where I attempted to hitch a ride to Elk Park. To set the stage for the rest of this saga, one should be aware that this Elk Park area is well reputed to be "hiker-unfriendly." Stories abound about an incident that took place several years ago, whereby hikers encountered fishhooks, strung at eye level, across portions of the trail. So, as we approached this area, it was with a healthy sense of paranoia.

I was not at all surprised as vehicles passed me by with my thumb dangling in the breeze. I finally gave up my attempts to hitch a ride and walked into a wind that brought tears to my eyes. Atlas, I spotted a small A-framed structure on my left, and from a distance I could make out a lighted sign advertising beer. I eagerly hastened my pace with the thoughts of food and sodas in mind. I made my way up an inclined dirt road and entered the establishment.

Behind a counter next to a drive-up window, sat a burley, bearded man dressed in hunting gear; directly in front of him, a large caliber rifle lay pointed towards the drive-up window. The bolt was open and a shell lay next to the chamber. I immediately sensed that I didn't want to linger long in this place; I gave the man my best good-ole-boy greeting. I believe it was something like, "Howdy neighbor." I was wearing my Army camouflaged cap, and hoped that this would help distinguish me from those "hippie hikers" that so often came through this area. I asked if he had food for sale, and he replied, "Nope, just beer." Foolishly, I then asked if he had any sodas, and he replied, "Nope, just beer." Can you believe that I asked this man a third question? "Is there a restaurant within walking distance from here?" He pointed in the direction that I had previously traveled before entering this man's domain, and he stated, "Up the road." I guess that I am a slow learner, because I asked him a fourth question, "Do you know if they are open?" He replied that he didn't know, and by now, I had run out of questions, so I turned and walked out of this beer joint in purest form.

As I left, I spotted a pay phone and attempted to call home; no one answered so I headed towards Elk Park; after a short distance I spotted the King of the Road restaurant on my left. There were no cars in front and it appeared to be closed. I went to the front and spotted a sign indicating that the restaurant operated Thursday through Saturday and opened at 1630. Guess what? Today was Thursday, and my watch indicated that it was 1530. Could this be for real?

In only one hour I could conceivably be setting inside this restaurant dining on some delicious, hot food. Wait a minute; this owner could be a relative of the beer joint proprietor. Nah! Not a chance… so I hoped. I set my pack down and reclined against the wall; it felt good to just set and wait for the restaurant to open.

It wasn't long before a man came to the door and invited me in. He was strikingly friendlier than I had expected. He offered me coffee and stated that the grill was not quite ready, but that I could go ahead and order. He recommended the 16 oz. sirloin steak and I immediately took him up on his suggestion. This turned out to be one of the best steaks that I had ever eaten; the Texas fries were a great compliment, not to mention the salad bar. The owner was a retired prison warden, and he and his son operated the restaurant on a part-time basis. He had just turned 62, and was ready to start drawing his social security pension. He seemed impressed that I was a year younger than he, and had plans to walk the AT to Maine. We both enjoyed our conversation and the waitress kept my coffee cup full; finally, I asked about desert. She recommended the homemade chocolate pie, and I asked for a plastic bag with which to carry the remainder of my steak back to the trail.

I was so full that I could barely waddle out the door. As I was about to sling my pack, the owner's son was leaving and he offered me a ride back to the trail. Can you believe this luck? By now, it was late afternoon and the skies were turning bleak. I thanked the young man for the ride and headed back to the Apple House Shelter that I had passed earlier in the day. I immediately got into my sleeping bag and dozed off for an hour or so. When I awakened, the shelter was full and snow was beginning to fall. We all talked for a spell while some cooked a late evening meal. Later that evening, I recited *"The Shooting of Dan McGrew"* for a weary bunch of hikers. (mile 380.6)

DAY 40 – April 18, 1997

We awakened to 1-2 inches of snow, and I was the first to depart the shelter. This would be a hard day of walking in fresh snow, especially on the downhill slopes. I kept changing outerwear … at first, I would be too hot, then too cold. As I made my way over the snow-covered hardtop leading to the wood line ahead, the white blazes were impossible to locate. The snow had obliterated the white trail markings on the pavement, as well as the trees. Barking dogs could be heard all about and this caused concern. I was glad when I located the double white blaze that signaled a turn for the next climb.

Whisper and I were the first in at Moreland Gap Shelter. This was the longest 14.1 miles that I have walked, thus far. The wind was fierce and blew directly into the open end of the shelter. I pitched my tent under some large pines and managed to stay dry and warm. I planned to do only seven miles tomorrow, and I planned come off the trail to spend the night in a hostel near Hampton. I need snacks, fuel, laundry, and most of all, a hot shower. I can't wait to get to Damascus and the prospects of warmer weather. This last 50 miles through the Roan Mountain area has been tough.

Still no sign of *Music Man*, *Sir Lancelot*, and the others. I sure am glad that I didn't take him up on the Kingsport side trip. I've heard that the bad weather caused some hikers to hold up at Overmountain Shelter. I'm apparently in a good seam as I move closer to Damascus. (mile 394.7)

DAY 41 – April 19, 1997

It snowed about two inches last night … nice, wet snow that slid off my tent with a gentle tap. I was up, fed, packed and ready for the trail before the kids in the shelter could get out of their sleeping bags. The trail was covered with the fresh snow, and occasionally, I looked back to view my tracks. It felt like a Christmas, and I was tempted to break out with a repertoire of carols; *"Winter Wonderland"* seemed most fitting. The hemlocks and spruce were heavily laden with fresh snow, and dipped their boughs as if attempting to block the trail. I took my walking stick and knocked the snow from the branches in order to stay as dry as possible.

I walked 5.6 miles to US 321 and 0.4 miles to Laurel Creek Hostel. I acquired a bunk space in a small four-person cabin near a stream. It was bitter cold and the unheated cabin mirrored the outside temperature. At least, I had a bunk and mattress, and I was sheltered from the biting winds. *Sir Lancelot* came in and we shared the cabin; *Dave* and *Beth*, the Quaker couple, occupied a cabin, and *Henny-Penny* and *Dear Heart* occupied another. I had a cheeseburger, coke and chips for $5. A single banana cost $.75, an instant oatmeal pack, $.75. I was aghast when they charged me $.38 oz. for fuel that we normally payed $.07 oz., or $1. for a full bottle. It was apparent that these people were not the norm when it came to hostel operators. We are about four days out of Damascus … more rain predicted for tomorrow. (mile 400.7)

DAY 42 – April 20, 1997

I left at 0807 and *Sir Lancelot* decided to sleep in. As I descended into Laurel Creek Falls, I was walking through some of the most beautiful country that I'd seen. The footing was treacherous at times, and I almost slid into Laurel Creek as I was traversing some slippery rocks that hung over the streambed. I would like to do this section, again, someday.

I arrived at Watauga Lake around noon and ate lunch at a lakeside picnic table. The shoreline was very cluttered, and I didn't filter water until I was well beyond the tributaries that fed the lake. It was a long climb past the Watauga Lake Shelter; I walked 16 miles in slightly over eight hours. I camped close to a spring while a few hikers went the extra 1.6 miles to Vandeventer Shelter. I laced my rice dinner with canned chicken and ramps ... so good. Arriving in Damascus was first and foremost on my mind. *Sir Lancelot* tented somewhere above me, out of site, thus living up to his reputation as a "stealth camper." (mile 416.7)

DAY 43 – April 21, 1997

What a way to begin the day; light rain, then thunder and lightening with spitting hail, as the temperature dropped by 20 degrees. I left camp at 0700 and ate lunch at Iron Mountain Shelter. Today, I took cover from lightening for the first time since departing Springer Mountain, GA. I removed my pack and nestled myself under some mountain laurel, thus avoiding any tall trees that might attract a lightening strike. In addition to hypothermia, lightening strikes were always a heightened concern.

As I continued, I saw one north-bounder on Iron Mountain, and a south-bounder at Double Springs Shelter, where I elected not to stay. I left the shelter when the rain had halted, but before I could get out of sight, a steady rain hit the area. It was only 1600 and I made a decision not to go any farther. This would mark the first time that I actually pitched my tent while it was raining. I had a mess for a while, but eventually got organized enough to fire my stove for the evening meal. It was beans and rice with ramps, followed by some chocolate pudding ... what a combination!

I dozed from 1800-1900 and then cleaned my utensils to make ready for next morning's fried peanut butter and jelly sandwich. I was only 18.2 miles out of Damascus, and I knew that I would probably not sleep well in anticipation of the next day's travel. I had planned to do about 14 miles tomorrow and camp on the outskirts of Damascus. This would allow me to take advantage of a full day when I reached one of the most popular trail towns on the AT. This was a strategy taught to me by my friend, *Sir Lancelot.* As expected, the thoughts of meeting Josephine, coupled with a Cracker Barrel breakfast, hindered my sleep. I was thankful just to be able to stay dry, as the rains pelted well into the night. (mile 433.0)

DAY 44 – April 22, 1997

Guess what? I was wide-awake at 0100 and couldn't go back to sleep, so I decided to go for Damascus. I packed up and was ready to leave by 0400. As I was about to level my tent, the bulb in my flashlight blew ... what a time for this to happen. I found my matches, an extra bulb, and somehow managed to rectify the situation with minimal difficulty; boy, was I ever relieved. The early morning fog bank was so thick that I could hardly see six feet in front of me, and I had difficulty in picking up a white blaze. I did pick up a blue blazed trail, and that only confused me further. I wandered about in a circle and then became concerned that I would lose track of where I had camped. I finally made it back to where I had pitched my tent. I discovered that I had camped right next to a fork in the trail that would put me right where I wanted to be. I learned a good lesson from this venture; before retiring for the night, always scout the area in search of the northbound trail blazes for the next day's journey.

With much relief, I departed the area and walked for 2.5 hours before I had enough light to see without using my flashlight. It sprinkled rain all morning and did not begin to clear until around 0930. I walked past the Abingdon Gap Shelter and set my mind on the remaining 10 miles. I passed one of the finest springs that I had seen on the trail, and filled my liter bottles without filtering the water. The remainder of the trail leading to Damascus was mostly rolling with few steep climbs. In fact, much of the trail was covered with pine needles, and that was welcome comfort to my tired, aching feet.

I arrived in Damascus at 1230 and walked past a city park to a bridge that would lead me down the main street to the Methodist hostel, The Place. As luck would have it, I found bunk space on the second floor. I showered, shaved, and hurried off to a local laundry to wash my filthy clothes and sleeping bag. I had a great cheeseburger and shake at the Dairy King while waiting on my laundry to cycle. When I returned to the hostel, I hung all of my wet tenting on a line and got myself situated in the bunkroom.

By now, the hostel was filling to capacity and *Sir Lancelot* had checked in. We went to Quincy's for supper; the food was outstanding and I felt full for the first time since I was at home for the Easter weekend. When I arrived back at the hostel, *The Spice Girls* and *Carrot Top* had moved into the other bunk spaces in the room. It almost seemed like a family reunion, as we all clustered in the common break area to tell war stories regarding our encounters of the past weeks. You could tell that confidence levels were peaking, as we celebrated our success of having made the 450-mile trek from Springer Mountain, GA. Approximately one-fourth of our long journey was now behind us. (mile 450.1)

DAY 45 – April 23, 1997

I awakened at 0400 and decided to start my day. Most of the hikers had plans to take the next couple of days off, and since I couldn't sleep, I set about doing some useful things. I polished my boots, shaved, and cleaned my pack; when I ran out of useful things to do, I went downstairs to the kitchen area and made some instant coffee. It seemed like the light of morning would never come, and when it did, the day was gray and overcast.

The Spice Girls had invited me to a pancake breakfast at Cowboy's, so I piddled around until they were ready. The blueberry pancakes lived up to the billing associated with their advertisement that we found tacked to the bulleting board. *Sir Lancelot* and I shopped at the local outfitters and just browsed around this quaint little trail town. The townspeople were very friendly to us hikers, as much of their economy depends on trail people. The new socks and inserts that I purchased made it feel as though I was walking on air.

Sir Lancelot and I returned to Quincy's where I had my first Calzone ... sort of a pizza looking fried pie. I topped this off with a pint of vanilla ice cream and some root beer. We then went to the Wednesday evening prayer service at the First Baptist Church. The marquee indicated that the service would begin at 1930, and when we arrived on time, we noted that the service seemed to be in full swing. We entered and took our places near the back of the church. Unbeknownst to us, the service had begun at 1900, thus the service for us lasted all of 16 minutes ... that had to be some kind of record. Several members came to us at the close of the service, and one of the elders apologized for the misleading time posted in front of the church. Even though the service was abbreviated, it felt good to be in church for the first time since Easter Sunday.

It was back to the hostel and time for that long awaited root beer float. I turned in at 2215, and the next morning *The Spice Girls* informed me that I had joined the ranks of a world-class snorer. They had attempted to record me, but had failed to charge their recorder batteries. (mile 450.1)

DAY 46 – April 24, 1997
Here I am, once again, awake at 0400. I sure hope that I can break this habit, especially when off the trail. After shaving, I loafed in the common area until 0600. I went back to Cowboys for another round of his delicious pancakes; they seemed even better this morning. You can tell by now that my thoughts are primarily occupied with talk of food. That is the natural outcome of food deprivation, and I'm sorry to report that this stayed with all of us until we reached the end of the trail; for 10 percent of us, this meant Maine.

This was the day that Josephine was to meet me and she arrived around mid-morning; was I ever glad to see her. I introduced her to as many hikers as I could find, and took her upstairs to view the bunk area where I had slept for the past two nights. She met *The Spice Girls* and *Carrot Top,* who shared the room with me. She seemed impressed? Most of the hikers were planning to move ahead today.

We stopped at a florist where I had ordered an arrangement to show my appreciation for all of her support. We were both tearful as we left town. We found a nice motel and went shopping for some clothing items that I needed. We had a great time and it would end all to soon. I knew that it would be harder to leave her this time than it was at Easter. We both knew that this would be the last time that we would see each other until I finished my journey in mid-September. (mile 451.1)

When I arrived in Damascus, I was fully aware that I had put the states of Georgia, North Carolina, and Tennessee behind me. Three down and only eleven more to go! Over the past 450 miles, many day hikers had asked me about my journey. I could recall in vivid detail my own disbelief when I first starting muttering, "Mount Katahdin, Maine," when asked about my destination. Reaching Damascus, Virginia was of immense psychological importance, and we all seemed to draw strength from one other, as if we had just been initiated into some sort of select club. During my stay at The Place, I had a conversation with *Ginger* who informed me that she and her partner *Nutmeg*, had informally voted me the "Most Likely to Succeed" out of the Class of '97. I reciprocated by thanking her for the vote of confidence, and stated that when I reached Mount Katahdin, the two of them would be standing with me.

DAY 46 – The Place, Methodist hostel, in Damascus, VA.

DAY 47 – April 25, 1997

We were just like two blubbering babies when Josephine dropped me off at the hostel. I hurriedly slung my pack and moved out without glancing back until I had walked a block or two. It struck me that this would probably be the last time that I would see her until I returned home in September.

I was leaving this quaint little trail town at 0815, and the American flag that I had purchased at the local hardware was snapping in the breeze. From this day forward, I would never be without Old Glory attached to my pack. I quickened my pace, as I followed the white blazed trail out of Damascus. Much to my surprise, *Sir Lancelot* had not departed with the others, and he caught up with me by mid-morning. The day was sunny, but rather cool when the sun slid behind the clouds. We walked 16 miles and stopped around 1700, just beyond Lost Mountain Shelter. I was ready to turn in by 2100 and planned to break camp early in the morning. *Sir Lancelot* liked to sleep in and I usually left camp before he was awake. Due to his long stride, he always caught up with me by mid-morning. By now, we had become good friends and respected each other's privacy. We seldom walked within site of each other, but managed to plan our destinations where we would camp. (mile 466)

DAY 48 – April 26, 1997

I broke camp at 0650 and headed for Mt. Rogers, the highest peak in VA, at 5,729-feet. As I made my descent along a winding path through a pasture, I sighted a road crossing that ran in front of a neatly kept white, clapboard house. I crossed a fence, and made my way across the road while looking for the white blaze that would lead me northward to Mt. Rogers. I had gone a short distance, when I spotted a walking stick leaning against a tree; probably deposited there by someone who came off the trail at the nearby road. Most thru-hikers walked with two fiberglass trekking poles, and they raved about how the poles took the stress off their knees, not to mention the extra balance provided when traversing rough terrain. Believe me, there was more than enough of that up ahead. I retrieved the stick, and cut it to match the length of the one stick that I had used since departing Springer Mountain. This would mark the last time that I would walk without the support of dual hiking sticks.

As I forged ahead, I wondered what kind of weather I would encounter on Mt. Rogers. The weather there was unpredictable this time of year and there had been an accumulation of snow two days ago. We were fortunate to miss the snow and were greeted by a mild, sunny day. We encountered lots of rock formations, and my feet felt stone bruised at day's end. We met several weekend hikers as we approached Mt. Rogers, some on horseback, but most on foot.

The privy near Saunders Shelter was something to behold; it had no roof and the sides were not high enough to lend total privacy to the occupant. I hesitated to use the privy, but nature called and I went for broke. As I sat scanning my trail data, some hikers came by and spoke; we all chuckled as they passed me by. I was beginning to sense that there was no place for vanity on the trail. The nearby shelter was a mess, as the wild ponies hung around to beg food from hikers. The front of the shelter looked like a barnyard, and you could see the remnants of gorp where hikers had fed the ponies.

We stopped after 15 miles, and pitched our tents on some very uneven ground. We were about to enter the fenced area, known as Grayson Highlands State Park. Wild ponies roamed throughout this area and a herd came through in the early morning hours; I shined my flashlight on them and they scampered. (mile 481)

DAY 49 – April 27, 1997

It rained most of the night; I packed my rain-soaked tent and moved out at 0700. *Sir Lancelot* never knew when I departed. As I entered Grayson Highlands State Park, the hazy fog made it difficult to see the white blazes at times. I had walked about 2.5 miles when I stopped to relieve myself; I had left my pack on the trail. The next thing that I heard was someone asking if I was Jim Richardson, known as *Easy Strider*? Scared me half to death! As it turned out, the person was a trail volunteer by the name of Ross Sherman from Wiggins, MS.

He informed me that my son was scheduled for emergency surgery on Monday, and I immediately knew that it had to be Chris. I pulled myself together and we both headed for his cabin that was located about three miles up the trail. As we walked past the next shelter, I informed one of the hikers that I was leaving the trail due to my son's impending surgery, and asked him to inform *Sir Lancelot* of my situation.

We hurriedly made our way to the cabin where Ross called the headquarters at Mt. Rogers Ranger Station, so that they could notify Josephine that they had located me. Ross' partner, Dean Sims, from Homestead, FL, was waiting for us, as Ross had radioed ahead that we were on our way. They offered me some coffee and made plans to get me to the Park Headquarters, so that I could call home and make arrangement for transportation. The two needed a supply pickup and decided to go now, instead of waiting later in the week.

Ross and I walked about 3 miles to his car on an old abandoned roadbed, and then it was on to the headquarters. I called home and Josephine informed me that our son, Mark, was already on his way to pick me up. Mark arrived around

1530, and we were home by 1830. I went directly to the hospital to see Chris and Dawn ... felt as if I was living in a schizophrenic world. I had traveled I-81, I-40, Boyd's Creek, Chapman Highway, and John Sevier Highway to reach University Hospital; a far cry from where I had begun my day on the AT ... welcome back to the real world! (mile 483.5)

DAY'S 50 thru 56 – April 28 – May 4, 1997

Chris underwent his third surgical procedure since January; I spent most of my time with Chris at University Hospital. He had such a difficult recovery and had tubes protruding from every orifice of his body; his weight dropped to 112 lb. before he was able to take solid foods. His daily oral intake consisted of ice chips to ward off dryness of the mouth. Throughout his long ordeal, Chris remained uncomplaining; he used the morphine drip sparingly and placed no demands on the nursing staff ... talk about a model patient.

When it was apparent that Chris was to be discharged, I began making plans to return to the trail. Josephine did not approve of this decision, as she had been stressed by Chris' medical condition as well as other circumstances.

Hindsight is always 20/20; if there was ever a time that I should have come off the trail, it was here and now. I suppose that my single-minded obsession with completing the AT in one season overcame sound judgment. This is a strong statement as to the value of a support system while on the trail. Someone had to step up to difficult challenges in order for me to realize mine, and that person was Josephine.

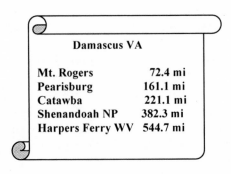

Damascus VA	
Mt. Rogers	72.4 mi
Pearisburg	161.1 mi
Catawba	221.1 mi
Shenandoah NP	382.3 mi
Harpers Ferry WV	544.7 mi

-5-

HIGHTAILING THROUGH THE HIGHLANDS
VIRGINIA/WEST VIRGINIA

> The state of Virginia holds more than 540 miles of the Appalachian Trail; this is more than the States of Georgia, North Carolina, and Tennessee combined. The trail snakes its way northward through beautiful, rolling pastureland before giving way to the more rigorous rock-faced climbs. The AT crosses the Blue Ridge Parkway more than 40 times prior to entering the Shenandoah National Park. This would be my favorite of the 14 states that I traveled through until I experienced Vermont.

DAY 57 – May 5, 1997
Josephine and I departed Seymour at 0500 for the long ride up I-81, where we backtracked through Damascus on Hwy 58 leading to Grayson Highland State Park. This would not be a pleasant trip. We said our good-byes, and I walked through a stable area that led to a pasture that would lead me back to the AT. When I arrived at the trail intersection, I discovered that I was now retracing my steps. I had walked 2-3 miles of this same section of the trail on April 27th.

The day was clear with a bit of chilling wind. I made my way northward knowing that my hiking group was at least eight days ahead. I resolved myself to the prospects that I wound never see them again. Dejavu ... I met Ross Sherman, the volunteer that had found me on the trail, at almost the same spot of our earlier encounter. We talked for a while and I learned that he had thru-hiked the AT in 1995, and that his trail name was *Mississippi*. I obtained his address and that of Dean Smith, so that I could write a note to their supervisor to acknowledge their commitment and service to us hikers.

I encountered only one other person on this day and that was a fellow hiker by the name of *Long Distance*. He was slack packing and walking south; his destination was the same as mine, only he had made arrangements to slack most of the way to Maine. The trail was very rocky, and I could tell a difference in my physical stamina following the eight-day lay off. I walked 19 miles and pitched my tent near a stream around 1600. I will walk the 20 miles to Mt. Rogers Recreation Area Headquarters tomorrow; this is where Mark had picked me up eight days ago. Today, I made a decision to change my trail name to *Reveille* in keeping with my military early rising habits. (mile 502.5)

DAY 58 – May 6, 1997

It rained last night ... getting good at packing a wet tent. As I made my way towards Mt. Roger's Headquarters, I met *Surf* and *Turf*, a husband and wife team from Georgia. *Turf* had fallen two days ago and busted her nose; the injury required medical attention at a local hospital and they had just gotten back on the trail. I immediately took a liking to the couple, and we walked together towards our mutual destination at the headquarters. Since I had already been to the headquarters, I knew that the rangers permitted thru-hikers to sleep on the open porch area on the backside of the building.

Several other hikers, to include *Henny-Penny* and *Dear Heart*, joined us there. One of the rangers was nice enough to leave the bathroom area open all night; I suppose the number of women in the crowd led him to this concession. A young couple and their dog slept next to me; can you believe ... the dog actually snored during the night. I suppose that this gives credence to the cliché, "dog tired." (mile 522.5)

DAY 59 – May 7, 1997

I departed the headquarters at 0600 on a day that would be clear and crisp. I soon came upon a hunter who was out for turkeys. He was well camouflaged and sort of startled me, as I almost walked upon him without notice. We talked for a while and then I continued towards the AT crossing at Interstate-81.

Just before I arrived at the Interstate crossing, I met a section hiker by the name of *Virginia Creeper*, who was heading in my direction. A southbound hiker had informed us that a thru-hiker from a previous year had left a $100. credit at one of the restaurants for the use of us aspiring thru-hikers. As I approached I-81, I saw two eating establishments and went to the nearest one; it turned out to be the wrong one, but I had a great meal with a milk shake.

The trail blazes were a little confusing after crossing the Interstate, and I ended up walking a mile or two out of the way before I regained my bearings. By this time, *Virginia Creeper* had caught up with me, and we walked the next seven miles together. He was good company and I discussed my recent ordeals with him, as we walked through some of the most beautiful farmland in Virginia. We ended up camping at Crawfish Valley, near a clear running stream. My little toes on both feet were hurting badly; I'll probably loose the toenails on my right foot ...hiked 18 miles today. (mile 540.5)

DAY 60 – May 8, 1997

I was on the trail by 0700 and left *Virginia Creeper* at the camp. He was only going another six miles, as his wife was coming from Richmond to pick him up. The weather was absolutely beautiful for the first half of the day. I walked through pastures of rolling hills that were breathtaking. At one juncture, I sat down on a grassy knoll and just soaked in the views of the far-reaching valleys. All of the farmhouses and out buildings were well kept and the red roofs set them off as if I was viewing a landscape painting.

As I proceeded to the next shelter, I met a father and son team who were experiencing the trail. The father had recently retired from the USAF and had plans to relocate to Virginia from Oklahoma. As I departed Knot Maul Branch Shelter, it began to rain, and I began to have thoughts of home and all that Josephine had gone through. It was during this time that I halfway made up my mind to leave the trail at Bland, VA. Somehow, the trail was beginning to loose its significance. I rationalized that I would have to come off the trail somewhere up the line, and that it might as well be now while I was within a reasonable driving distance from home. What had begun as an inspiring day had quickly turned to one of despair. I tented a short distance from a road crossing and didn't feel comfortable; however, two section hikers from Alabama were camped a short distance up the trail. (mile 554.4)

DAY 61 – May 9, 1997

As I left camp, the skies were threatening and the footing on the trail matched the bleakness of the forthcoming weather. I navigated the huge rocks and boulders overlooking Burke's Garden. It is speculated that this valley was formed by a meteor strike that took place millions of years ago. The gigantic boulders surrounding the trail gave credence to the magnitude of that awesome impact; the valley is referred to as, "God's Thumbprint."

Rain and wind were the order of the day, as I pushed on to Jenkins Shelter. It was there that I first met *Farmer-Dan*, a retired farm agent, who was headed for Maine. We chatted as we ate, and I left the shelter at 1400 on my way to the highway leading to Bland, VA. On the way, I met a troop of wilderness hikers, comprised of several teenaged boys and their youthful counselors. The boys appeared none too happy with their excursion, and you could hear them coming up the trail several hundred yards before I met them face-to-face. I soon came to an area where the trail split; signs marked an alternate trail as "high water" route. I decided to stay on the white-blazed trail, as my goal was to stay as pure as possible on my journey to Maine. It seemed as though I had dismissed, at least for the moment, the very real prospect of leaving the trail at Bland. I tented in a briar patch next to a spring-fed lake. It rained all night and the winds were fierce, as I hunkered down for the night. (mile 563.4)

DAY 62 – May 10, 1997

I broke camp at 0645 and walked the seven miles to US21/52 that led to, either Bastian or Bland. I chose to head eastward towards Bland, and tried hitching until it became apparent that I wasn't going to have any luck. I walked the 2.8 miles into Bland and ate breakfast at a convenience mart before moving on to a motel on I-77. The walk from town to the motel added another mile. As I crossed over the Interstate, an elderly couple passed me as they made their turn at the exit. I sensed that they saw me as a weary, homeless vagabond who had been traveling the Interstate ... I chuckled to myself and continued on my way.

I checked in, took a quick shower, and then proceeded to lay out my wet gear as best I could. I hand washed my clothes in the bathtub and strung a line at the back of the motel. I walked back into town to shop the local IGA and purchased a new American flag at the local hardware. That evening, I ate supper at a nearby Dairy Queen and called home. I explained my plan to leave the trail to Josephine, and she encouraged me not to do so. Chris was progressing well, and I sensed that she was managing well without me. I never really wanted to give up on the trail, and this turn around made me feel a little better about leaving her to handle all of the daily burdens that she had to shoulder.

All in all, my stay in Bland was not a memorable one; the motel owner seemed to be resentful of hikers, as a result of his bad experience with some previous hikers. The townspeople that I met seemed none to friendly, and face it, I probably wasn't in a good frame of mind to begin with. (mile 570.4)

DAY 63 – May 11, 1997

Before leaving the motel, I ran into *Surf* and *Turf*. They had arranged for a ride back to the trailhead at 1000, and asked me if I wanted to join them. What they didn't tell me was that the man who was to transport us charged $5. per head for the 2.5 mile ride back to the trailhead. Not knowing this, I went back into town for breakfast and a gentleman next to me offered me a ride that I turned down, as I didn't want the couple to be delayed should they attempt to locate me. I was a little put out with this situation, but I just chalked it up to experience.

The morning sun felt good, as I departed for Jenny Knob Shelter. I arrived there before 1700 and pitched my tent behind the shelter. Tomorrow would be a full day, as I plan to do 20 miles to Woodshole hostel. (mile 582.6)

DAY 64 – May 12, 1997

I left Jenny Knob Shelter at 0637 and walked alone most of the day. Today, I met *Paratrooper* for the first time; I didn't realize it then, but we would become the best of friends in the months to come. He was setting beneath a tree next to the trail resting before the next steep climb. He complained of indigestion and I located an Alka Seltzer in my pack and gave it to him. He and I walked together for the remainder of the day.

We ran into Tillie Wood and her friend, Juanita. Tillie and her husband, Roy, settled in this area in the early 1940's. Roy was Deputy, Secretary of the Interior, and set about studying the elk population. Following his death, Tillie maintained their 1880's farmhouse and converted and old barn into a hostel to accommodate hikers. Woodshole is one of the most popular hostels on the entire trail. A former thru-hiker by the name of *Highpockets* has become a permanent caretaker, and stays there to care for the property while Tillie returns to her Atlanta home in the off season.

After stowing our gear in the barn's loft, I signed up for Tillie's famous set-down breakfast that would be served in the log farmhouse the next morning. *Highpockets* maintained a solar shower, and the common area of the barn housed a refrigerator stocked with sodas and candy. One could take items of choice for $.50 and it was run on the honor system. This hostel was a prime example of one that was run out of altruism and kinship with the thru-hiker. This was in stark contrast to the hostel back in Hampton, TN. The loft was soon full of hikers, and we each had a twin-size mattress for a bed. At day's end, *Paratrooper* and I, along with seven other hikers, were bedded down and eagerly anticipating tomorrow's breakfast. (mile 601.8)

DAY 65 – May 13, 1997

Paratrooper and I left about 0905 in a light drizzle; it rained most of the morning and the downhills were as slippery as they were steep. We were headed to Pearisburg, VA, where we hoped to find bunk space at the Catholic hostel. We hit the hardtop leading into Pearisburg around 1400 and began our journey into town.

We had walked most of the three-mile distance to the hostel, when a man in a pickup truck stopped to offer us a ride. He was a medical doctor who had been visiting patients at one of the nursing homes. He was a hiker in his own right, in addition to being a member of the Holy Family Church, where we were headed. We were grateful for the ride and joked that we must have looked pretty bushed for the doctor to take the time to transport us to the hostel. We found bunk space on mattresses that lined the loft area of this cabin-like hostel. The church took great pains to accommodate thru-hikers, and a retired Army person was in charge of maintaining the hostel.

We walked back into town to do laundry, eat, and purchase food for our continued journey the next day. I had lost a spring bar from by watchstrap and located one at a jewelry store. When I returned to the hostel, I microwaved some pizza rolls, and had my usual milk and cookies, topped off by a pint of B&J ice cream. Most of the hikers that I had met at Woodshole congregated here for the night.

Later that evening, I was surprised to see *Kampfire*, the nomadic trail helper that I had met at Nolichucky Campground back in Erwin, TN. He was soliciting hikers to return to Damascus for the forthcoming annual event known as Trail Days. I was to learn that many of the younger hikers did return to Trail Days and then were shuttled back to the trail after a two to three day festive break; this gave me a chance to make up some ground and maybe catch up with my original group. (mile 612.2)

DAY 66 – May 14, 1997
I left the hostel before 0700 heading to town for coffee; I located an ATM and checked out my balance before going to the Post Office to mail some unneeded items home. A kindly, older gentleman offered me a ride back to the trailhead and I respectfully declined. I was still determined to do this trail in the purest sense. As I departed town, I had a difficult time picking up the white blazes. In retrospect, I wished that I had taken the gentleman up on his offer of a ride

The weather was nice when I left, but that didn't last very long. I was walking in a steady downpour by 1000. By the time I reached Ricefield Shelter, I had all of the fun that I could stand for one day. Around noon, five other hikers arrived; I really wanted to move on, as the day was still young. As I waited for a lull, it became apparent that none of us were going anywhere soon, as the wind and rain only increased. I ate my evening meal and sought comfort in my sleeping bag as the temperature dropped; could this really be the middle of May? The rain and wind pelted even harder during the night, and we all hoped for a better day tomorrow. (mile 619.0)

DAY 67 – May 15, 1997
I departed the shelter at 0700 … a little cool, but no rain. The early morning walk was pleasant with some prospectively good views that were obstructed by dense fog. I bypassed the next two shelters in hopes of making it to a campsite near a spring.

This afternoon was a real challenge, as the trail was so difficult. I met *Laughing Matter* heading south on her way to Pearisburg. She had been slacking with *Long Distance*, and had made plans to return for Trail Days. I couldn't help thinking of *Kampfire's* parting words back at the Catholic hostel, "See you face

42

down on the streets of Damascus." I was sure that Benton McKeye, the progenitor of the AT, would have rolled in his grave had he been aware of how Trail Days had degenerated into a drunken street party by a distinct minority of thru-hikers. I'm still 60 miles out of Troutville where I planned to resupply and spend a night in a motel.

The trail beat me down, and I pulled up 2.5 short of my planned destination. I tented on a hillside near a trickling branch, and as I prepared for bed, I could hear the rain pelting my tent. The wind picked up to the point that I was concerned that it might pull my tent stakes out of the rain-saturated ground. I hunkered down and managed to stay warm, as the wind howled and the temperature plummeted. (mile 631.9)

DAY 68 – May 16, 1997

Surprise! I awakened to snow and ice all **about** me. The wind had blown snow against my tent, and the condensation from by body heat had caused my tent to ice over. I fired my stove for some oatmeal and coffee, and dreaded to break camp. I shook off most of the snow and ice, and crammed the tent into my trusty plastic bag; was this heavy gauge plastic bag ever a lifesaver. It was around 40 degrees, but the wind chill made it feel much colder.

I walked from 0800-1000 in my heavy rain gear, as my fingers actually turned blue. When I finally reached the lower elevation, there was no snow or ice and the temperature had moderated. I walked through rolling pastures, and passed a herd of cattle that stood motionless, as they curiously watched me make my way past them through the mushy trail.

When I reached VA 42, I decided to walk 1.6 miles off the trail to a country store that was listed in my trail guide. After walking for a good 2-3 miles, I was able to find a person pulling out of a driveway, and asked him for directions to the store. He informed me that the store had closed last year; he graciously offered me a ride and I hopped in the back of his pickup for a ride back to where I had begun "the chase." I had consumed all of my water and could not arouse any of the local inhabitants to see if they might give me some water. It was apparent that some of these people had been disturbed enough by streams of hikers who traversed this very isolated area. A young man in his teens approached me, and I asked if he knew where I might get some water. He attempted to knock on some doors, as he was familiar with some of the locals; he had no more luck than I.

I crossed a stile and headed northward in search of water. This was a beautiful area, but it was now somewhat tainted by my misguided trek in search of the country store, and the lack of success in garnering some much needed water. It was not long before I came to a stream that seemed none too inviting, as it looked to be snake infested. I cautiously made my way through a briar patch down a steep embankment to filter my water. I was glad to finally be back on the trail; I tried to forget the dismal events of the day. I pitched my tent around 1730 and was asleep by 1930. Tomorrow has got to be a better day! (mile 652.1)

DAY 69 – May 17, 1997

I hit the trail at precisely 0700; I walked 18 tough miles over several rock faces and plenty of uphill climbs. I never saw a soul until I met four southbound section hikers. This is the third consecutive day that I have not seen a northbound hiker. I continue to be in a pocket somewhere between the original group and the hikers that I had recently met. The white blazes were difficult to locate on one particular section. I was glad to meet the aforementioned south-bounders who affirmed that I was on the right footpath.

As I made my way up Brushy Mountain, I was eager to reach the site where Audie Murphy had died in a plane crash in 1971. In addition to being an actor, he was the most decorated soldier of WWII, and a member of the 3rd Infantry Division. When I was an 18-year old private, I had visited his old unit, Co. B, 15th Infantry Regiment, at Sandhill, Ft. Benning, GA; I was a member of his old regiment at the time. I stopped at the memorial and took a picture; the morning sun was warm and the skies were a powder blue. All this was in stark contrast to my aching feet, especially my little toes on both feet. I pitched my tent near Pickle Branch Shelter. With any luck, I'll be in Catawba tomorrow. (mile 670)

DAY 70 – May 18, 1997

I began a long, but pleasant walk over some spectacular rock outcroppings known as Dragons Tooth. The climbs were very strenuous, and at times, the downhill were even more challenging. There were places that one might have fallen, thus ending any chances of reaching Mount Kathadin, ME. Today, I met *Mother Hubbard*, a lady in her early 60's, from New York. As I continued, I met *Southpaw* who had hiked one-half of the AT in 1996. He turned out to be one of those people who couldn't get the trail out of his system. He lived in nearby Catawba Valley, and frequently hung out on this section of the trail. We talked for a while, and he really seemed to enjoy talking with us north-bounders. Furthermore, he delighted in providing refreshments for us hikers when we reached the parking area on VA 624. I located the cooler of sodas next to his car, and downed the first soda that I had had since leaving Bland; I could get used to this "trail magic."

After a short break, I walked a short half-mile until I reached VA 311,

44

where I stopped at the Catawba Grocery. I drank a quart of whole milk, and ate a half box of chocolate chip cookies. I called Josephine and then walked 2.3 miles eastward to The Homeplace Restaurant. It was Sunday and this farmhouse restaurant was bursting at the seams. The after-church crowd was dressed in their Sunday finest. As I made my way up the long driveway, I was more than a little conscious of my appearance. I off-loaded my pack near one of the gazebos, and made my way to the covered porch. While I was waiting for my table, *Southpaw* drove up and let *Mother Hubbard* out. She had some difficulty traversing the downhill rock formations, and he had accompanied her off the mountain, and deposited her at one of the most storied eating establishments on the trail. The owners were hiker friendly and even provided a trail register for us to sign. *Mother Hubbard* and I sat down to a family style dinner, second to none. What a feed ... chicken, country ham, 5-6 vegetables, homemade biscuits, preserves, lemonade, and finally, cherry cobbler topped with ice cream. You guessed it; I ate too much and almost got sick ... I never regretted it, though.

We left the restaurant and walked a half-mile to another country grocery store, where I purchased some snacks for my continued journey. *Mother Hubbard* decided to stay at the store in a little cinder block storage building that was available to thru-hikers. As I walked past the Catawba Post Office, the country store, and the long winding road leading to the former Catawba Hospital, I reminisced about the year 1973. I had turned down a job offer at the hospital, and remembered just how disappointed our two older sons had been at not being able to move to this beautiful valley.

I moved on and walked with *Stringbean,* who had just returned to the trail after having attended Trail Days back in Damascus. This would mark the first time that I had encountered any of my original group. The gradual climb out of this valley was a welcome venue, as I was full to the gills. I tented at 1630 ... filtered my water for the next day and turned in early. Oh yes ... I had carried a chicken breast and a couple of biscuits from The Homeplace, and that topped off the end of a very good day. (mile 682.9)

DAY 71 – May 19, 1997

I broke camp at 0600 and walked to McAfee Knob, one of the most photographed spots on the AT. I walked the steep grade to Tinker Cliffs with three hikers that I had met back in Hot Springs, NC. The greater Catawba Valley was something to behold; I knew that I would want to return to this area at some future date.

I didn't intend to walk the 20 miles to Troutville, but I had consumed all three liters of my water, so I decided to go for it. I was glad that I did as I found a nice Howard Johnson motel room with a guest laundry; being able to wash my filthy clothes was becoming almost as important as eating restaurant food ... well, almost as important. I shopped a Winn Dixie and ate at Burger King. I plan to eat breakfast at Shoney's tomorrow before I depart. So much for tomorrow ... right now, I was enjoying my great motel room, and most of all, the hot soak baths. It was raining, as I turned in for the night; although I was surrounded with all the amenities of home, I was restless and didn't sleep well. (mile 704.3)

DAY 72 – May 20, 1997

I walked the mile round trip to Shoney's and consumed the long anticipated AYCE breakfast. I located fuel at another close by motel where several other hikers had stayed and departed Troutville around 0930. I had to stop and put the cover on my pack due to a light rain; the rain stopped in about an hour and the remainder of the day's walk was delightful. I walked past two shelters and camped just south of Bobblets Gap Shelter.

I crossed the Blue Ridge Parkway for the first time five miles west of Peaks of Otter Recreation Area. The trail crossed the Parkway at several junctions and I frequently saw and heard vehicle traffic, as I walked on extremely rocky footing beneath the roadbed. Spring was in the air and the traffic hummed like a swarm of bees. It seemed a little strange to be so close to civilization after walking for countless days without the awareness that there was still a very busy world, just beyond the footpaths of the AT. I stopped at 1800, after walking 18.2 miles and ate a light supper. I turned in at 2000 with plans for another early morning departure. (mile 720.5)

DAY 73 – May 21, 1997

I was on the trail at 0700 and stopped at Bobblets Gap Shelter for water. I was met with the barking of a trail dog, owned by *Vagabond*. She and a homeless person by the name of *Bean* had spent the night at the shelter. It was obvious from his attire that *Bean* was not a thru-hiker. While *Vagabond* got her dog under control, I filtered water from a boxed spring. I moved on, but before I did, I asked her if she was ready to move on. She stated that she was planning to leave the shelter later in the morning.

I stopped at Cove Mountain for a lunch break, and she and her dog came in, as I was about to depart. She indicated that she had been somewhat leery of *Bean* at first, but after talking to him last evening, she had felt at ease. As it turned out, he had gotten on the AT on February 13th near Gatlinburg, TN, and would get off the trail from time-to-time in order to earn enough money to resume his travels. We talked for a while and I sensed that she was not long for

46

the trail, as she was having problems with her water filter, pack, and boots. I learned later on that she had left the trail near her home in Washington, DC. I moved on as the weather was perfect for walking ... just enough wind to evaporate the perspiration, but not brisk enough to chill.

I pushed on to Bryant Ridge Shelter about one mile north of VA 714. Much to my surprise, *Bean* was at the shelter, as he had gotten a ride shortly after leaving Bobblets Gap Shelter. He had an acquaintance that lived in the area, and this person had transported him to a nearby town for resupply. He planned to spend three days at the shelter before resuming his travels. He turned out to one of the more interesting people that I would encounter on the trail. He related that he had left home at age 16 and had been on the move ever since. He was very intelligent and related numerous experiences to include his adventures in Alaska, where he had worked as a cook for the Alaska pipeline. He had little formal education, but was a voracious reader and was quite familiar with the works of Robert W. Service, the bard of many poems and ballads concerning the gold rush of the Yukon Territories. When he learned of my fascination with Services' works, he asked me to receipt a piece. As he followed me back to the trailhead, I receipted *The Cremation of Sam McGee.* He replied, "That was wonderful." We wished each other luck as I moved on. As I neared the trailhead, I met *Vagabond,* and she was planning to spend the night at the shelter. I walked for another hour and a half before tenting next to the trail. I had a New Orleans gumbo dish laced with a can of minced clams that I had purchased in Troutville. Oh yes ... I spotted a bobcat on the trail today ... it was stalking a field mouse when I startled it. The cat ran into the bushes and the mouse ran for cover in a hollow log. I laughed at the very thought that I had actually saved a mouse from certain disaster, considering how much I detested the little vermin's domination of the trail shelters. (mile 733.8)

DAY 74 – May 22, 1997

I left camp at 0630 ... it was cool enough for a windbreaker, but clear and sunny. I stopped in at Cornelius Creek Shelter where two section hikers were just getting up at 0830. I used the privy and pushed on to Thunder Hill Shelter where I stopped for a noonday snack. As I was leaving, a young kid by the name of *Four Winds* came in. He had attended Trail Days and seemed to delight in telling me about some rowdy hikers being arrested in Damascus.

I walked alone to Marble Springs campsite where I set up camp at 1630. Later, three other hikers came in and it was good to have company; I've been alone for the past three nights. The weather report indicates clear weather through Memorial Day weekend. (mile 751.2)

DAY 75 – May 23, 1997

I broke camp and was on the trail by 0640. It's a beautiful day and my heels are not hurting as badly, today. I walked through miles and miles of blooming rhododendron; the sweet aroma took my mind of my aches and pains. I felt stronger today than any other day that I could recently recall. The afternoon trail was mostly uphill, but only for short intervals ... some rocks, as usual ... they really take a toll on your feet. I stopped at the gravesite of a small child by the name of "Little Ottie," who died in this area after wandering from the family home place.

I walked 19.1 miles by 1630 and stopped at Punch Bowl Shelter. Two southbound section hikers came in behind me and tented next to the pond. Legend has it that the pond is haunted by the ghost of "Little Ottie" who supposedly makes appearances on rainy, foggy nights. I was much less concerned about the prospects of a ghost than I was about the ferocious mosquitoes that took no mercy on us sweaty, grungy hikers. Water was hard to come by, and I vowed that I would not under any circumstances filter from that stagnated frog pond. I scouted about and located a slow running trickle that seemed to feed the pond. It wasn't the best, but I boiled the water for my evening meal.

At dusk, I was the only person in the shelter. The area around the shelter was uneven and soggy, so I decided to break a cardinal rule and sleep in the shelter in lieu of pitching my tent. I had the shelter to myself, except for the mice and mosquitoes. The mice prowled all night and the constant croaking of the frogs gave them competition for annoyance. I pitched and turned all night. If "Little Ottie" had made an appearance, I most assuredly would have seen him, as I seldom slept for any length of time. I was anxious for the light of dawn, as I knew that the next day would find me arriving at VA 60, where I hoped to find a country store and some goodies. (mile 770.3)

DAY 76 – May 24, 1997

I left the shelter at 0645 and set a good pace towards VA 60. I sat down in a parking area next to the highway and a gentleman in a pickup approached me to ask if I needed a ride. I was delighted by his kind offer and he drove me the 1.2 miles to Hamm's Country Store. The store was reputed for keeping erratic hours, and I felt fortunate to find them open for business; the owner lived in the back of the store. They had little that I needed, except for sodas, cakes, and candy ... of course, they had plenty of beer, but no milk, bread or sandwiches, as the deliveryman had passed them by earlier in the week.

I made my way back to where I had crossed VA 60 and proceeded northward. The next three hours were spent climbing Cold Mountain that reminded me of the balds of North Carolina and Tennessee. The temperature was in the 80's with little wind. I met seven day hikers, but no thru-hikers. Once again, I sensed that I was in the middle of my old gang and the new gang that I had walked with out of the Mount Rogers area. I'm averaging 15-20 miles per day without discomfort, although my right heel continues to be sensitive … so what else is new? The Rhododendron and Laurel blooms are at their peak and the sweet aroma does wonders for my mental outlook. I sing a lot on the trail and this seems to help keep my mind off hunger; I stay hungry all the time and when I'm not eating, I'm thinking about eating. I crave milk and ice cream most of all while chocolate chip cookies run a close second.

I tented at a place called Hog Camp Gap near a creek, so I had plenty of water. I must have bypassed the campsites that were annotated in my *Data* Book. The area where I pitched my tent was probably one of the poorest sites that I had ever selected. The field mice were so numerous that I couldn't leave my tent flap open for a second without a possible intrusion. I felt distraught by my blundering campsite site selection and settled in for a long night. (mile 786.8)

DAY 77 – May 25, 1997

I was up before daylight and left camp at 0640. I backtracked to the spot where I had veered off the trail. I headed north over grassy balds and caught up with the three section hikers that I had met yesterday. I was really dejected when they related how their day had ended yesterday. Instead of chasing some obscure campsite, they proceeded into the bald area where some weekend campers had offered them fried chicken, potato salad, and all the good things that usually accompany a family outing. I could hardly believe my errant judgment in camping at that mice-infested site last evening … oh well, lighten up … things could be a lot worse. I ate lunch at Seeley-Wordsworth Shelter and moved on to The Priest Shelter; the shelter looked so deteriorated that I moved on after filtering some water. I was looking forward to reaching VA 56 at the Tye River, where I hoped to acquire enough food to get me to Waynesboro.

As this was Memorial Day weekend, I met several section hikers, as well as day hikers. It was here that I met a nice couple that was section hiking. Crystal was an aspiring author who hoped to soon publish her first novel; Kevin was a ship captain who sailed out of West Palm Beach, FL for ports at Jakarta, Grenada, and other exotic destinations. They had been hiking parts of the AT since the late 1980's and jokingly stated that they hoped to complete the entire AT by the year 2015. They were impressed with my having carried an American flag on my pack since departing Damascus. They indicated that another hiker, who also carried the Stars and Stripes, had passed them. I didn't realize it at that time, but this was none other than my buddy, *Sir Lancelot*. The rains came once again, just after I had pitched my tent. I met lots of nice people today. (mile 803.5)

DAY 78 – May 26, 1997

It was raining hard when I broke camp at 0600 for the slippery, downhill descent to VA 56. I began my day with a very hard fall on the rain-slickened rocks. I picked myself up, wiped off the mud the best I could, and proceeded with caution. I had gone only a few hundred yards when I took another spill; I couldn't believe that this had happened. To this point, I had taken only one hard spill, and that was way back at Neels Gap, GA. Oh well, no real harm done, except for my pride; I didn't realize it, but this would be only the beginning of many more falls before I would reach Mt. Kathadin in Maine.

It rained even harder as I cautiously made my way to the parking area alongside VA 56, where I had hoped to hitch a ride to C & C Grocery. I was soaked to the bone and equally as chilled. My attempts to hitch were for naught, so I resolved to walk the three miles to the store, hoping with every step that they would not be closed for Memorial Day. The way that my day had begun left me with the very real prospect that the store's owner would be celebrating the long weekend like so many others. As I approached the store, I held my breath in hopes that my worst fears would not come to fruition.

Glory be … C & C Grocery was open! This little country store served as the Post Office for the community of Tyro, VA and carried a variety of food and hardware for the local inhabitants. The Campbell's were hiker-friendly people and treated us with respect; some stores in rural areas are not quite so receptive to "hiker trash." I consumed a microwave sandwich that was none too tasty, but I didn't much care. I gorged on pastries and milk and set about restocking my diminished food supply. I even purchased a can of Treet, the only canned meat on their shelves. Now one has to be hungry to go for Treet, which I consider to be at the very bottom of the food chain … directly beneath Spam. Anyway, I packed it away for later consumption back on the trail; I had my usual pint of ice cream and waited for the rain to let up.

By now, some of the locals had assembled at the store and I met a 94-year old gentleman who seemed to be in amazingly good health. He related that he had lived in the mountain area where I had just passed through. I wished that I had taken more time to talk with him, but I needed to get back on the trail. A man in his early 40's offered me a ride part way back to the trail, and I gladly accepted his offer; these extra off-trail miles were beginning to add up. I crossed a footbridge over the Tye River and began my ascent towards the summit of Chimney Rocks and Hanging Rock Overlook. I stopped at Maupin Field Shelter and quickly decided to bypass this gloomy shelter after attempting to dry my tent on a hastily strung line.

I walked until 1800 and ended up at Cedar Cliff overlooking the Sherando Lake Valley. I tented near a rock cliff overlooking a dairy farm deep in the valley. I cooked the evening meal on a rock cliff and watched the sun set with a real sense of satisfaction that this day had turned out so well, given the way that it had begun. I went to sleep listening to the sounds of bellowing cows. (mile 821.1)

DAY 79 – May 27, 1997

I left my campsite at 0613 under cloudy skies; the moisture hung overhead like a cloak … lots of rocks, rocks, and more rocks. I met a southbound hiker from Indianapolis, by the name of *Half-Way*; he was a second year pre-med student who had gotten on the trail at Harpers Ferry, WV. He was passing out surveys to thru-hikers regarding the state of their health. He planned to follow up by inquiring about the hiker's health upon completion of the trail. I agreed to participate in his research and took a survey sheet with me.

I walked slightly over 12 miles to the intersection of I-64/Blue Ridge Parkway, where I stopped at the Information Center to inquire about directions to Waynesboro. I planned to get a motel room and resupply for the trek through the Shenandoah National Park (SNP). As luck would have it, a female volunteer at the Center was going off duty and offered me a ride into Waynesboro. I was grateful for this five-mile ride into town and this "trail angel" gave me a tour of the town before dropping me off at the Comfort Inn. She also stopped at a local outfitter on the way to conduct some personal business, thus affording me an opportunity to purchase a lightweight rain jacket; I sent my heavier rain jacket home. The rains of the past week were burdensome and it didn't take me long to decided that I needed more than one night off the trail to rekindle my dampened spirits. (mile 833.2)

DAY 80 – May 28, 1997

I stayed off my feet as much as possible and lounged around the motel area that was very convenient to the downtown area. I went to Weese's, a renowned restaurant, for AYCE pancakes and had a large pizza for supper. I am eating so much more now, sometimes eating when I really don't need to; it's amazing what deprivation can do for one.

I visited two churches in the vicinity to see if they had Wednesday evening services; much to my surprise, they didn't. Mid-week services had been discontinued during the summer vacation months due to dwindling attendance. What's the world coming to? I sat by the pool and soaked up some sun while planning my next venture through the SNP; the restrictions placed on hikers in the park are very stringent, some would argue, to the point of ridiculousness. I planned to stay at the motel as long as possible tomorrow. I didn't realize at the time, but too much time off the trail tends to break one's sense of focus. I would learn this lesson later on up the trail in MD. I lost count of my hot soak baths and for the first time, I actually watched some TV; could this be a sign that I was beginning to soften? By days end, I had thoroughly convinced myself that I had needed the two days off. Today I met *High-N-tite* and *Struggles*, two kids from New Hampshire who were walking home. (mile 833.2)

DAY 81 – May 29, 1997

I departed Waynesboro earlier than expected after running into *B'ama* who had stayed at the Comfort Inn where I had spent two nights. He had garnered a ride back to the AT with a gentleman from Ellijay, GA near Springer Mountain, where we had begun our journey back in March. This gentleman was very familiar with the AT and seemed to enjoy talking to us, as we made the five-mile ride back to the trail.

We walked the Skyline Drive to the entrance of the SNP, where we registered at a Ranger Station, and followed a blue blazed trail to the AT. The regulations in SNP were numerous, and according to all of the trail data literature, rigorously enforced. The last thing any of us wanted was to be fined, or worse, banished from the park. I went ahead of *B'ama* and arrived at Calf Mountain Shelter at 1115; I decided to hold up there. One could not tent in the SNP unless the huts were full. This would be my first exposure to bear poles that were located along side the huts. You should have seen us hikers making our first attempts to hang our food sacks on these poles.

It was cloudy and cool as the late afternoon approached. I had sent my winter sleeping bag home, as I planned to use a fleece-like blanket that I had purchased in Waynesboro. Several hikers would stay here tonight, as this was a jumping off place for the rest of the journey through the SNP. I planned to move through the Park as quickly as possible, as I was anxious to reach Harper Ferry, WV. *B'ama* did not come in and this caused us concern. We later learned that he had decided to forgo the difficult trail, and instead, walked the paved highway through most of the SNP … oh well, to each his own. (mile 840.1)

DAY 82 – May 30, 1997

I left the shelter at 0640 … it was very cool and cloudy. The terrain seemed to be somewhat better as I entered the SNP. I met two section hikers from Gray, TN, by the names of Sam and Dave. They were headed south and I never encountered anyone heading north. I crossed the Skyline Drive on several occasions, and stopped off at Lofton Mountain Campground Store for some snacks.

I moved on to a campsite off the AT; it was difficult to tent, as one had to be aware of all of the stringent rules of the SNP. I startled a deer just before stopping for the day. A doe and her newborn were headed towards me. I could see that the fawn was still wobbly, and I moved off the trail to let them pass. The doe nudged her newborn off the trail into some thickets; she then circled around me and stopped under a tree next to the trail. I moved ahead, and as I passed the fawn, it lay trembling in the underbrush. If I had not known where to look for the fawn, I would have passed it by, as it blended perfectly with the underbrush. The doe returned to reclaim her offspring. I marveled at the animal instinct that I had just witnessed. I walked a bit farther before pitching my tent and hung my food 10-feet off the ground, as this was bear country. I thought of the fawn and realized that its chances of survival were precarious, at best. I walked 22.5 miles today. (mile 862.6)

DAY 83 – May 31, 1997

It rained all night and it was difficult to break camp in the early morning mist. I was wringing wet by 0930, and walked for hours before I met anyone on the trail. I did get a pleasant surprise on this rainy day, as I came upon some sodas on the trail. Later in the day, I met a couple that had thru-hiked the AT in 1995; they gave me an apple and a candy bar, and wished me well.

According to the shelter register, *Music Man* is just ahead of me. *Sir Lancelot* and *The Spice Girls* are about 3-4 days ahead … sure wish that we could link up again. The sweltering humidity and the steep climbs took their toll on me today. I stopped at 1800 after walking 11.5 miles. I planned to do 15 miles tomorrow, and make my way out of the SNP as soon as possible. I am now in the area where the two female hikers were murdered last year. The women, who are now walking this section of the trail, do so with a healthy degree of concern. Rumors abound regarding the particulars of the slayings and to this day, remain unsolved. (mile 873.1)

DAY 84 – June 1, 1997

I broke camp at 0650, as it began to rain hard; it wasn't long before the rain came down in torrents. I arrived at Lewis Mountain Campground and made my way to the camp store. It was only 0830, and the store didn't open until 0900. I called Josephine, and while we were talking, *Music Man* arrived with his wife and son. He had taken a two-day break from the trail to spend time with his family. He had jumped ahead in order to reach Lewis Mountain Campground, and planned to go back and slack the 17 miles. He and I rented a small hiker cabin that slept four people. Jim, the manager of the camp store, was very helpful and we were appreciative of the cabin. We purchased some wood for the stove and prepared chili and hotdogs for the evening meal.

Soon after, *High-N-tite* and *Struggles* arrived and shared the cabin. We split the $15 fee four ways and settled in for the night, as the rain continued to fall in torrents. The wind and rain added to the chill of the cabin and it didn't take long to burn the first bundle of wood. The two kids purchased another bundle, and we all were in our sleeping bags early. We were hoping for a break in the bad weather; regardless, I planned to walk tomorrow. (mile 886.2)

DAY 85 – June 2, 1997

It was 0650 when I left *Music Man*, *High-N-tight*, and *Struggles* at the hiker cabin, and headed out in a driving rain. I walked hard and fast on fairly level terrain ... some up hill, but only for short distances. I got off for lunch at Wayside Visitor's Station and had a great cheeseburger. *High-N-tite*, and *Struggles* came in behind me; these two kids from New Hampshire set a torrid pace, somewhere around 3-4 miles per hour. I moved on with them in the lead, and they would stop for smoke breaks so that I could catch up with them. They always stated that they were "just resting," in order not to make me feel bad for not being able to keep up with them. We made the next nine miles in record clip, at least for me.

We passed a riding stable and knew that it couldn't be far to Skyland Lodge, and their much-acclaimed restaurant. We hoped to be able to find reasonably priced lodging. We arrive at 1600 and rented a one-room cabin with three twin beds. Talk about good luck ...we got the last available overnight accommodation. We hung our wet gear on the railing of the front porch, showered, and made our way back up a long winding footpath to the restaurant. The dinner was the best that I had partaken of since leaving Waynesboro. When we arrive back at the cabin, we discovered that field mice were not necessarily just a trail shelter nuisance. Mice had found their way into our packs and had already eaten some of *High-N-tite's* snack food. All through the night, the mice ran rampant, and we slept in fitful bursts, anticipating the worst when we awakened in the morning. (mile 903.2)

DAY 86 – June 3, 1997

We had a good breakfast at the lodge and before departing, I ran into *Carrot Top* and *Grump,* who were slacking through the SNP. *Grump's* mother had previously hiked the entire AT, and she was providing the transportation for their slacking endeavor. The two kids left at 0830, and I hung around until 1000 in hopes that the rain would subside. *Carrot Top* and I left together, and I was only going nine miles to the next shelter. After a short distance, she went out ahead of me, as she was not carrying a pack and could make better time. The weather was horrible ... cold, and damp, with a mist that seemed to hang at tree top level. There was little hope of seeing the sun on this day. I did not venture out to the overlooks, as there was absolutely no prospect for a view of the valley below.

I was glad to arrive at Pass Mountain Hut, and decided not to pitch my tent since no one was at the shelter. Anyway, I would have been in violation of SNP regulations had I pitched my tent when the shelter was not full. I was glad to put this short day behind me. The rains were beginning to dampen my spirits, as well as all of my gear. The dampness permeated the open hut, and I was beginning to wonder about my decision to send my winter sleeping bag and heavy gauged rain jacket home. It was not long after retiring that I realized that the fleece-like blanket that I purchased in Waynesboro would not suffice. I spread my nylon tent over me, so as to retain enough body heat in order to sleep ... tomorrow has got to be a better day. When I settle in tomorrow night, I hope to be only 2.5 miles out of Front Royal, VA. (mile 913.9)

DAY 87 – June 4, 1997

I departed the hut in a heavy mist, but the rains seemed to be lifting. The sun broke through around mid-morning, and I stopped a short piece off the trail at Big Meadows Wayside; the place was empty except for a few employees. The food was adequate, and I was most thankful to be out of the elements for a short while. I ran into *Carrot Top* and *Grump* on two occasions today; they seem to enjoy slacking and plan to do so all the way to Harpers Ferry, WV. I walked past Mary's Rock, a much talked about viewing spot; the fog banks were so heavy that I would not have been able to see anything ... so much for the scenic beauty of the SNP.

By now I had only one thing on my mind, and that was the Tom Floyd Wayside Shelter that would be my overnight stop. Front Royal, VA and a Shoney's AYCE breakfast, also lay heavy on my mind, not to mention a motel room. The foul weather has stopped a lot of hikers, and I was beginning to sense that the hiking crowd that left Springer Mountain was beginning to thin out. I was glad to arrive at this fairly new shelter that had a nice deck attached to the front. I cooked the evening meal and settled in for the night; looks as if I'll be alone tonight, except for the mice, of course. (mile 937.6)

DAY 88 – June 5, 1997

I awakened this morning to a surprise! Of all things, some kind of varmint chewed through the tongue of my right boot, and chewed the tops of both boots. I can't wait until I get home to bait some traps! Later, I would to learn that the culprit was probably a porcupine, and not a mouse; I still "hates meeces to pieces!"

I departed the shelter at 0630 for the short walk to US 522, where I hoped to hitch a ride into Front Royal. The trail was overgrown with shoulder high saw grass. I was absolutely drenched to the shoulders when I finally arrived at the highway. I tried hitching for approximately 30 minutes, with no luck. After a short while, a car drove up from the direction of Front Royal and stopped near the trailhead. *B'ama* got out for his northward journey on the AT. I was surprised to see him, and to learn that he had beaten me to Front Royal by at least a full day. With a sheepish grin, he informed me that he had been walking the Skyline roadway most of the way through the SNP. It didn't seem to bother him that he was not hiking the white blazed AT. It would bother me immensely to call myself a "thru-hiker," and not stick to the AT footpath. Oh well, he wasn't the only, so-called, thru-hiker to do this. *B'ama* was at least honest about his short-circuited adventures.

The person that had dropped him off was the owner of a motel in Front Royal, and he offered me a ride for $4; I was glad to finally be heading into town. I rented a room at his Center City Motel that turned out to be a shabby room with messed up plumbing and a missing window panel in the bathroom.

I walked to the downtown area and ate at McDonalds ... no Shoney's in this town. I visited three Christian bookstores, and picked up some inspirational cards for handout on the trail. It was here that I met a nice lady by the name of Maggie Sill at Heaven Sent Bookstore; she gave me a WWJD bracelet that I would wear it for the remainder of my journey. Later this evening I would open my door to find that *Paratrooper* was occupying a room next to mine; was I ever glad to see him, again! We made plans to have breakfast the next morning, and coordinated our schedules so that we could link up again on the trail. One of his daughters was coming to Front Royal to pick him up for a visit with her in DC. He had five daughters, and this was only one of several off-trail stops before he would reach Mt. Katahdin in the fall. He and I are very compatible and we both looked forward to meeting again. (mile 940.7)

DAY 89 – June 8, 1997

Paratrooper and I had breakfast at a pancake house restaurant. I replenished my fuel and headed back to the trail around mid-morning. Since I was getting such a late start, I decided to pay the motel operator to take me back to the trailhead.

The trail was overgrown much like it was from Tom Floyd Wayside Shelter to US522. This section of the AT was the worst maintained trail that I had encountered since departing Springer Mountain on the 10th day of March. The trail was extremely rocky, and I was not beyond complaining to myself, as I trudged along. I hiked a little over 15 miles to Dick's Dome Shelter, a 12-foot geodesic-dome structure, built in 1989. I was to spend the night alone, once again ... seems as if I'm still in a pocket between both groups that I have walked with. The shelter was located beside a stream and dampness permeated the shelter. I had Harpers Ferry, WV on my mind, and I would be glad when morning broke so that I could move on. (mile 956.2)

DAY 90 – June 7, 1997

Up and out at 0645 ... the trail began with a moderate grade for the first 5-6 miles, where it abruptly turned into the hardest section that I had encountered in a long while. I met the Potomac Appalachian Trail Club (PATC) maintenance supervisor and the president of the club, who were out on a trail inspection hike. The trail supervisor had a pleasant Australian accent, and he and the others passed me heading northward to their destination at the Blackburn AT Center. I would meet them again the next day, when I stopped in at the Center for a break and some lemonade that they provide for hikers.

I would walk 19 plus miles today before reaching my destination at Bears Den Hostel. I tented on the grounds for a fee of $6. That included a shower, washer/dryer, and use of the kitchen area. My plan for the next day was to move on to Blackburn ATC that lay 7.8 miles ahead. This will leave me 11.8 miles out of Harpers Ferry, WV ... I'll be there on Monday. (mile 974.8)

DAY 91 – June 8, 1997

I arose at 0400 and went to the hostel community room, read a newspaper, and drank some good coffee for a change. I departed Bears Den Hostel at 0640 on my way to Blackburn ATC; I arrived around 1100 and partook of their lemonade. I walked another 3.5 miles to David Lesser Memorial Shelter; had to walk another 0.5 miles downhill to a spring to get some water. I had met *Yahoo* and *Father-Time* earlier in the day, and they had just stopped in for some water.

On their way to the spring, *Yahoo* shouted, "snake!" *Father-Time* reached into the brush and pulled out a 6-foot rat snake, and proceeded to toy with it before turning it loose. The snake headed in my direction before veering off the trail into the heavy brush. I knew that the snake was not poisonous; nonetheless, I didn't want anything to do with snakes. *Father-Time* grew up in the mountains of northern Georgia near Dahlonega, and he was no stranger to all kinds of snakes. They got their water and moved on to Harpers Ferry, while I decided to hold up at the shelter and make Harpers Ferry tomorrow. (mile 985.9)

Tomorrow, I will set foot in the state of West Virginia which has only 2.4 miles of AT within its boundaries. As I look back on my journey through Virginia's 544 miles of AT, I do so with a great deal of fondness, even though the past forty days were tainted with snow, ice, fog, and the seemingly never-ending rains. I flushed quail, grouse, chipmunks, deer, snakes, and a bobcat without sighting a single black bear. I believe that I was the only thru-hiker that did not see black bears through the Shenandoah. I will never forget the rolling pastureland of southwest Virginia, and the neatly kept farm dwellings with their brightly painted red roofs. The many food outlets along the Skyline Drive were of immense benefit to us always-famished hikers. The AT crossed the Skyline Drive more than 40 times in a 100-mile stretch. On some days, it was possible to eat two meals at restaurant outlets along the trail. The towns of Bland, Troutville, Waynesboro, and Front Royal provided me with motel accommodations that helped rejuvenate my dampened spirits. Who could forget the little country stores that stocked only a few staples for the locals. To us weary travelers, they were viewed as mini-supermarkets, as we replenished our food supplies with Snickers, cookies, fried pies, oatmeal, cheese, and peanut butter. Of course, we downed all of the sodas, B&J ice cream, as well as any other junk food that could possibly provide us with the fat calories that we so desperately needed. With all of this behind me, I was filled with an overwhelming sense of confidence as I neared the historic town of Harpers Ferry. I knew at this juncture that I would reach Mt. Katahdin, barring any serious injury that would force me off the trail.

DAY 92 – June 9, 1997

Up and out early for the short 9-mile trek to Harpers Ferry. I arrived at the Appalachian Trail Conference Headquarters around 0845, where I signed in and had my picture taken for the conference scrapbook. My package from home that included a new pair of boots and a lightweight sleeping bag was awaiting me at the headquarters. This was an early Father's Day gift from my family. I got a nice room directly across the street from the headquarters. Al and Allison Alsdorf, who proved to be great hosts, operated the Harpers Ferry Guest House B&B. Allison did a load of washing for me and went out of her way to make me comfortable. These kind people make a journey such as this worthwhile. I had a private room with adjoining bath and kitchen privileges; I felt right at home.

I ate dinner at the local Ponderosa Steak House and I really gorged myself; I returned full to the gills and wrote some post cards before retiring for the night. I sensed that I would have a difficult time leaving all this great company. I was so excited about approaching the 1,000-mile mark that I found it hard to sleep. Tomorrow, I will mail by varmint-chewed boots home and be on my way. Maryland, here I come! (mile 994.8)

DAY 93 – June 10, 1997

I departed the B&B around 0930, and walked past a burned out church on the way through the old city of Harpers Ferry, where Josephine and I had visited last October. It seemed like only yesterday that she and I had walked the exact footpaths. As I proceeded out of town, I sensed the historical significance of this area. Just think ... John Brown, the abolitionist, had attempted to capture the federal arsenal here in 1859, and here I was, treading on the same soil. I proceeded across the Goodloe Byron Memorial Bridge, where I turned right onto the C&O Canal towpath, and walked the three miles that bordered the Potomac River.

The honeymoon was soon over, as I found myself back on the usual climbs. Today was clear and a little warm ... nonetheless, a great day for walking. By day's end, I had walked 17.1 miles to Dahlgren Backpackers Camp. This was the only place on the AT with state-provided showers. I was the only person to camp at Dahlgren this evening. I took advantage of the hot showers and tented close to the restroom area to take advantage of the lights. I had a certain uncomfortable feeling while camping alone at this facility, as it could easily be reached from a nearby highway.

Tomorrow, I will set my sights on Pen Mar County Pavilion near Cascade,

MD; our oldest son, Brent, and his family resided there while he was stationed at Fort Ritchie. I was hopeful that *Paratrooper* would catch up to me fairly soon, as I planned to stop over at Fort Ritchie for a couple of days. (mile 1,001.7)

Harpers Ferry WV

Cascade MD	40.2 mi
Mason Dixon Line MD/PA	40.4 mi
Pine Grove Furnace	
State Park PA	78.2 mi
Duncannon PA	123.6 mi
Port Clinton PA	193.9 mi
Delaware Water Gap PA	272.3 mi

-6-
ROCKY ROAD AHEAD
MARYLAND/PENNSYLVANIA

DAY 94 – June 11, 1997
I broke camp at 0645 and had good trail until 1000. The rocks reminded me of VA, yet I knew that the worst was yet to come in PA. My feet were beginning to feel the pain of breaking in my new boots. I walked through Washington Monument State Park and stopped there for a snack break after locating a soda machine. This interesting historical area's centerpiece was a rugged stone tower dedicated to the memory of George Washington. The tower rises to a height of 34 feet, and was erected by the citizens of Boonesboro on July 4, 1827. I wondered if our son, Brent, had spent some time here while on a family outing when he was stationed at nearby Fort Ritchie, MD.

I met several southbound hikers today, but no one heading north. Being alone gave me plenty of time to reflect on life's situations. I crossed over Ritchie Road, and knew that this road would lead me to the front gate of Fort Ritchie. It was all that I could do to muster enough determination not to get off the white blazed AT, and "cheat a bit," by walking the hardtop road. I walked a steep uphill grade for a mile or so, and then a steep downhill to the spring at the base of Devil's Racecourse Shelter. After one glance at this primitive shelter, I looked for a tent site. The shelter was damp and very much over used; it reminded me of a stable, as the maintenance crews had scattered straw on the floor to soak up some of the moisture. There was no suitable ground for tenting, so I reluctantly settled into a corner of the shelter. My new, lightweight sleeping bag proved to be very warm, as I settled in for the night.

I was awakened at 2130 by two hikers who arrived in a huff. These two were something else ... they stripped to the bare and went to a stream for a quick bath. *Houdini* needed to be at Mt. Katahdin by the third week of August in order to return to his teaching job. His partner, *Possessed*, was a 63 year old retiree, who seemed to be running himself into the ground, following the torrid pace being set by his partner, who was at least 20 years his junior. I didn't sleep well after being awakened by the commotion, but tomorrow night I would be in the guesthouse at Fort Ritchie, that is, if there should be a vacancy. (mile 1,029.8)

DAY'S 95/96 – June 12-13, 1997

The early morning air was crisp and the skies were blue; I was filled with jubilation as I arrive at Pen Mar Pavilion by mid-morning. I took a break at the picnic area and located the attendant who gave me directions to Fort Ritchie. I attempted to hitch a ride with no luck, but I didn't care, because I knew where I was going and I didn't mind the 3-mile walk to the Army base.

After presenting my ID card to the MP at the entrance, I passed through the arched gate and walked straight to the guesthouse, where I inquired about accommodations for the evening. A young lady by the name of Donna was attending the desk, and she informed me that there had been a cancellation at Lakeside Lodge. What a break ... this accommodation was in the old Officers Club that had been closed, and my suite had been one reserved for visiting field grade officers. The suite was available for only one evening and I rejoiced at my good fortune. I checked in and surveyed my kingdom. Would you believe that I had a setting room with refrigerator, microwave, and a sofa that swallowed me. This room was off the master bedroom with a private bath. Could I have died and gone to heaven?

Following a shower, I made my way to the bowling alley where I ate a late morning breakfast. I shopped the commissary for food and visited the barber for a "high and tight" ... boy, did I ever get scalped. As if I hadn't walked enough, I decided to stroll around the lake and just soak up some memories of past visits at this base, the best-kept secret in the Army. I felt sad knowing that this would be my very last opportunity to stay at Fort Ritchie, as the base was scheduled for closing in October 1998. I called home to inform them of my great fortune.

I awakened the next morning and was greeted by threatening weather. I checked with the desk clerk to inquire about cancellations, as I relished the thought of staying another day and night at the base. I was trying hard to convince myself that I really deserved a two-day respite. No luck this time ... I packed up and was ready to head to the bowling alley for breakfast when it came a downpour.

I had taken cover under the front canopy when the clerk came to the door to exclaim that there had been a cancellation at the guesthouse. About this time, the Housing Manager came out of the lodge and offered me a ride to the guesthouse; I couldn't believe my continued good luck. He deposited my gear and me in front of the guesthouse and I checked in.

I spent the day rambling about the base and even walked another six miles in order to take a picture of our son's former residence. At day's end, I was totally satisfied, as I retired for the evening. Already, I was dreading the thoughts of getting back on the trail. Could this stay really have softened me to this point? I knew that I had to move on tomorrow! (mile 1,029.8)

DAY 97 – June 14, 1997

Got to get moving again … boy, my motivation has taken a nosedive! I felt a certain amount of sadness as I made my way back up the 3-mile winding road to Pen Mar Pavilion. I arrived around 1000 and made my way to a picnic table near the concession area and purchased a coke for the trail that lay ahead.

Much to my surprise, *Paratrooper* came up the trail and we greeted each like two long lost brothers … was I ever glad to see him. He told of his visit with his daughter in DC and how he had been doing big mileage days to catch up with me. Much to my disappointment, he was only going 3.5 miles up the AT where he planned to get off the trail, again to visit with another daughter. As we walked together, I joked with him about all of his side trips, and wished that he would run out of daughters soon, so that we could finish the trail together. We walked only 2.4 miles until we reached the Mason Dixon Line that separated the states of MD and PA; good-by grits and never-ending refills of coffee and tea. *Paratrooper* left the trail at PA 16 where he would link up with his daughter.

I proceeded another 12 miles before putting up at Jim Thorpe Shelter. There was no water at the shelter and I had to walk at least 0.5 mile to a paved road to locate a spring. A couple and their 10 year-old son were setting along the road where I filtered water from a spring. They asked questions about my journey and marveled that I was traveling alone. I made my way back to the shelters; this was the second time that I had run into dual shelters, each sleeping 10 or more. I was the only one to stay the night. I suppose that the distance to a water source discouraged the others.

I settled in for the night and made plans to hike 23 plus miles tomorrow in order to reach Pine Grove Furnace State Park; this would mark the halfway point of my 2,160-mile journey. *Paratrooper* planned to be back on the trail by Sunday. (mile 1,050)

DAY 97 – Crossing the Mason-Dixon Line at MD/PA border.

DAY 97 – Waking up alone at Jim Thorpe Shelter in PA.

DAY 98 – June 15, 1997

I awakened alone and was on the trail by 0620. I enjoyed the early morning walk and met several day hikers who were out for the weekend. I ran across *Cub* and *Kitt*y, two very unlikely hikers. They seemed to be struggling along and had stopped to cinch the ropes that were holding their sleeping bags on their backs. They related that someone had stolen their packs, food, and necessary equipment at a state park. They had been given sleeping bags, rope, and foam padding back at Vision Quest, an outdoor wilderness camp; at this juncture, they had only a single ration of food between them. I had enough food to get me to Pine Grove Furnace State Park. I gave them several rations and they seemed appreciative. I also gave them one of the inspirational cards that I had been handing out on the trail and moved on.

As I came to a road crossing, I began to feel badly about not sharing some coffee and candy bars that I was carrying. I remember glancing at my WWJD bracelet, and it didn't take long to figure out that I needed to share more with this couple. I filled a plastic bag with the aforementioned items and deposited the bag with a note on a tree stump in the middle of the trail.

I would cover 23 miles today and the walking was not too difficult. I encountered lots of downhills with a few steep climbs, and I was grateful for the light breeze. I arrived at Ironmasters Mansion Hostel around mid-afternoon. The mansion was built in 1827 and served as the home of the ironmaster of the Pine Grove Furnace Ironworks. The ironworks made cannonballs during the Revolutionary War and was also served as an Underground Railroad shelter for runaway slaves. There was only one southbound hiker who had checked in ahead of me. I'd finally reached the halfway point on the trail … could this be true?

Tradition called for thru-hikers to consume a half-gallon of ice cream in one setting; I was only too glad to oblige and ordered what turned out to be a very dry cheeseburger and washed it down with a soda. I carried the half-gallon of butterscotch ice cream back to the hostel and made my way to a picnic table where I proceeded to honor the long-standing tradition. I was a little surprised that this unusual combination did not make me sick; what a turn around from my earlier experience with food on my climb out of Georgia. The lady and two young sons that managed the hostel were very nice and the eight year old showed me to my quarters; I gave him a tip and he retreated with a broad smile.

This old mansion had a very interesting history and I felt privileged to be staying here for the night. The $14. fee included a fix-your-own pancake breakfast the next morning; I dozed off thinking of a triple stack with lots of syrup. In my excitement, I almost forgot that this was Fathers Day. I planned a lazy 15-mile trek for tomorrow. (mile 1,073)

DAY 99 – June 16, 1997

As I made my way down a path to the hardtop that would lead me to the AT, I was stopped by a thru-hiker named *Chicken Little*; he asked that I take his picture in front of the mansion. He and I would become good friends as we moved up the trail.

On the outskirts of the park, I located the signpost marking the official halfway spot on the 2,160-mile Appalachian Trail. I set my camera on automatic shutter and recorded this memorable occasion. I signed the log with the scripture, *"I can do all things through Christ who strengthens me,"* Philippians *4:13.*

The next 10 miles proved to be relatively flat terrain followed by five miles of boxcar-sized boulders. When I arrived at Alec Kennedy Shelter, I met Jerry Huffman, a data analysts, from the DC area who spends his annual vacation time section hiking the AT. Just before dusk, we heard the crowing of a chicken making its way to the shelter; it was none other than, *Chicken Little,* who turned out to be quite a comedian. He kept us laughing until 2200 when I finally fell asleep. We made plans for our next day's journey to Boiling Springs, PA. (mile 1,088.5)

DAY 99 – Leaving Ironmasters Mansion Hostel.

DAY 100 – June 17, 1997

We were on the trail by 0630; it was good to have early morning company, as I am usually alone when I break camp. *Chicken Little* and I soon pulled ahead of Jerry who was getting off the trail at Boiling Springs, PA. We walked through miles of corn and wheat fields and on one occasion we missed an obvious white blazed turn, thus we walked at least two miles out of the way. We ate wild strawberries and blueberries as we moved along the trail. *Chicken Little* was always looking for a photo opportunity. He shot everything in sight, to include a dead chipmunk that we pretended to eat; that says something about our sense of humor.

We arrived in the quaint, little town of Boiling Springs around 0830. We stopped to talk with two men who were fishing in a pond in the middle of a park. They were amazed that anyone would set out to hike 2,000 miles, let alone with 50 plus lb. strapped to their backs. We moved to US 11 where we hoped to find food at a truck stop. As we crossed the overpass bridge spanning the highway, we could see several businesses to our left. We made our way along this heavily trafficked six-lane highway and walked for at least two miles until we reached the Flying-J-Truck Stop. Low and behold, the Country Market Restaurant and Buffet was located in the complex. Talk about good food ... we practically foundered ourselves and departed with full stomachs and high spirits.

I had shared some personal testimony with *Chicken Little* regarding my blessings on the trail, and how I had been influenced by my contact with Maggie Sill at her Christian bookstore back in Front Royal, VA. He asked for her phone number, as he wanted to purchase several of the WWJD bracelets to hand out on the trail. He seemed genuinely moved by my experiences and we often talked about our faith as we moved forward.

We walked 19.2 miles before I decided to camp beside a small stream. He decided to move on towards Duncannon where he was expecting to pick up a new pair of boots that his wife was sending. We agreed to link up in Duncannon and continue our journey from there. My feet were really bothering me today ... I am ready for a good nights rest and anxious to reach Duncannon tomorrow, where I hoped to pick up a mail drop from home. (mile 1,107.7)

DAY 101 – June 18, 1997

I broke camp at 0648 and it began to rain shortly, thereafter. The trail was fairly steep and the rocks were difficult to maneuver. The morning air was very heavy as I hurried towards Duncannon. I passed Thelma Marks Shelter to my right and did not stop until I came to a very steep turn on the trail. I paused to get my bearings as I found it difficult to pick up the white blazed trail.

Finally, I located a white blaze that wound to the right and headed out. I walked for about an hour when much to my disgust, I came upon a sign to my left, leading to the Thelma Marks Shelter. I could hardly believe my eyes! I had backtracked on the southbound AT and had not picked up any landmarks until I had come upon this shelter sign ... talk about feeling disgusted! I quickened my pace towards Duncannon, almost running, at times. This was one trail experience that I would not share with any of my fellow hikers. Of course, many of them had probably made miscues such as this during their journey.

I stopped at the spot where I had gone astray, took off my pack and set about looking for the northbound blaze that I so desperately needed. I finally located the trail that had cut back sharply to the left and headed straight down to the town of Duncannon. I arrive there shortly after 1230 and made my way towards the main street, and the renowned Doyle Hotel. The Doyle was built around the turn of the century by the Anheuser-Busch family and served as the hallmark stop over for thru-hikers.

I entered the bar at the Doyle and there stood *Chicken Little* who bought me a soda. What a place! I secured a flophouse room from the bar waitress whom served as the room manager and made my way to the third floor to find my room. I removed the padlock on the door and cautiously entered the room. On my left, an antique chest of drawers … an iron bed with coiled springs directly ahead … dirty, soiled, carpet on the floor … and, best of all, a corner room with two windows, but no screens. Could life get any better than this? I made my way down a hallway to the community bath; you guessed it … claw-footed tub and matching commode. All that I wanted was hot water for my bath, as there was no shower. Only the brave of heart, or the sorely deprived would have ventured one step into that bathtub, but I did, as I was sorely deprived! After sorting my dirty clothes, I made my way back to the bar where I had a delicious cheeseburger. The bar served as the main dinning outlet in this little river town and the food was actually very good. I located the town's only laundry and proceeded to do my washing. This would be my first and only experience, whereby the coin changer gave back .95 cents for the dollar bill. Several teens hung around the streets and I wondered how they would escape this environment, as there seemed to be so little for them to do, except hang out.

By the time that I arrived back at the Doyle, the weather was looking foul. The bartender reported that a severe storm front was predicted to move through the area, but *Chicken Little* decided to move on anyway. The bottom fell out shortly after he left. I wondered how he would fare with his new boots after they became water logged. As thunder and lightening sounded all around, I was thankful for having a room that would at least protect me from the elements … or, at least, I hoped that it would! To be truthful, I wouldn't have missed this hotel experience for the world. What a town … frozen in the 1940's like so many PA towns … flags everywhere, as patriotism abounds throughout the area.

Before retiring for the evening, I found a convenience store and purchased some additional food for tomorrow's journey. The clerk was very friendly and talked of her concern for the youngsters of the community, as they had virtually no recreational outlets. The store would open at 0500 tomorrow and I would have my early morning coffee there. (mile 1,118.4)

DAY 102 – June 19, 1997

While at the Doyle, I met *Harry-Carry*, a schoolteacher from PA, who was on his third thru-hike of the AT. He had stayed at the Doyle for two nights attempting to shake a rattling chest cold that had plagued him for over a week. I also ran into *Top-Cop*, a retired highway patrolman from PA, and he asked how my son was doing following his surgery. He was the hiker who offered to pray for Chris' recovery when we first met at Mt. Rogers Ranger Station, where I had come off the trail to return home. He stated that he had been praying everyday for Chris, and he rejoiced in the fact that he had made a full recovery and was back at work.

I had a great stay in Duncannon and didn't leave until around 0930. On my way out of town I walked a back street just to soak up the atmosphere of this quaint little river town that time has forgotten. My feet seemed light as I made my way to Clark's Ferry Bridge that spanned the Susquehanna River, the widest and longest river crossed by the AT. While I didn't realize it at the time, this would be only one of many great rivers that I would cross; namely, The Connecticut, The Potomac, The James, and The Hudson Rivers.

As I made my first steep climb after crossing the river, I took one last glance back towards Duncannon. I moved forward for the next 11.1 miles and stopped at Peters Mountain Shelter. *Harry-Carry* was already situated for the evening and I decided to join him. It wasn't long until *Houdini* and his partner, *Possessed*, arrived in their usual huff. They had gotten off the trail back in MD to attend a family reunion and were once again setting a torrid pace in order to complete the trail by late August. This was my second encounter with them; they stripped to the buff and proceeded to search out a nearby water source. ... these guys must have been nudist.

Top-Cop came in next and lamented about his stay at the Doyle Hotel. He was not nearly as impressed with the spartan atmosphere as I had been. The shelter was fairly new and spacious with a unique table for cooking. I stirred up my usual rice dish and added a can of chicken for a gourmet meal. That evening was the first in many days that I settled in without rain, or the threat of rain forecast for the next day. I enjoyed the company and felt good as I turned in for the night. (mile 1,130.1)

DAY 103 – June 20, 1997

I departed the shelter at 0710 and walked with *Houdini* for the first six miles; his partner, *Possessed* followed. *Houdini* was a Christian Scientist, and we shared religious philosophy as we walked. He believed that we are all capable of controlling most everything that happens to us. He discounted my excuse for snoring, when I characterized the annoying habit as an involuntary body response. I didn't argue the point, but I still firmly believed that us snorers really have no control over this response.

We took a break at a road crossing near a running stream where *Houdini* waited for his partner to catch up. He invited me to join them for a steak cookout, as *Possessed's* wife planned to meet them a short distance up the trail. I respectfully declined and moved ahead to Rausch Shelter, where I would encounter a south-bounder by the name of *Merlin*. He had gotten on the AT in New York and was headed as far south as his legs would carry him. He wore a broad brimmed hat with a turkey feather attached to the band. In real life, he was a magician who made his living performing with various troupes around the country; Florida seemed to be his main domicile. He performed magic rope and card tricks for me and amazed me with his slight of hand. I cooked dinner with him at the shelter and decided to pitch my tent a few hundred feet behind the shelter.

Top-Cop came in before we had finished our evening meal and settled into the shelter for the evening. This shelter had a running water trough directly in front and the water was clear and very cool; I filtered my water and turned in for the night. This day had been an interesting one, and I really enjoyed the mix of people that I had encountered today. (mile 1,147.7)

DAY 104 – June 21, 1997

I departed Rausch Gap Shelter at 0640 heading for 501 Shelter. I missed a white blazed marker and walked two or three miles out of the way. I finally got my bearing and soon came to a little country store at Green Point, PA. Just my luck ... it had gone out of business, but the phone booth was still in operation. I called home to let Josephine know where I was. She seemed so overwhelmed with holding things together that I offered to come off the trail. In comparison to her plight, completing the AT seemed rather insignificant at this time. I resumed my walk and after about 200 yards, I sat down under the shade of some cedar trees and prayed about what I should do. I vowed to make a decision by the time that I reached Port Clinton.

I arrived at the 501 Shelter at 1630 and settled into the fully enclosed structure run by George and Joan Shollenberger. They sold ice cream and sodas out of their home that was located only a few hundred feet from the shelter.

George had rigged a solar shower nearby and we were able to bath for the first time since leaving Duncannon. (mile 1,165.6)

DAY 105 – June 22, 1997

I left 501 Shelter ahead of the others, as I needed time by myself to contemplate, whether or not, I should leave the trail and return home. I sat down at an overlook and turned to *I Corinthians, Chapter 13*, which had kept running through my mind for the past several days. After several minutes, I had my answer. I could no longer let my self-pride keep me away from home. Josephine needed me more than I needed the trail. I felt at peace with my decision.

The remainder of the day remained a blur, except for the hard spill that I took during an afternoon thunderstorm. I had gashed my left shin and elbow when I fell on a very rocky portion of the trail. The deep cut on my shin would have qualified for stitches if I had been near a medical facility. I finally got the bleeding stopped and made my way to Eagle's Nest Shelter, where I pitched my tent. After supper, I decided to use the Crazy Glue that I had carried for boot repair to suture my cut; it worked and I often laughed at my first aid technique. That night, as I lay in my tent listening to my radio, I heard Michael Bolton's, *Go the Distance*, and it brought tears to my eyes, as I knew that I could go the distance, if only I wasn't needed at home. (mile 1,179.8)

DAY 106 – June 23, 1997

I left ahead of the others heading to Port Clinton where I would spend an exasperating day making plans to return home. I walked into this quaint little village founded in the late 1700's on the Schuylkill River. I made my way to the town pavilion that was sponsored by a local church. It was here that I met Robert Breon, a church elder, who ministered to hikers by providing water and transportation to Hamburg, the nearest town with accommodations. He invited me into his home where I met his gracious wife, Helen. They offered me the use of their phone so that I could inquire about bus transportation for my trip home. This couple would turn out to be the most inspiring of all the many wonderful people that I would encounter on the trail.

Two of my hiking buddies, *Paratrooper* and *Chicken Little,* came in and we accepted Mr. Breon's offer of a ride into Hamburg, where I would proceed to purchase some decent clothes for the ride home. I gave away most of my provisions as I seemed totally resolved to leave the trail. I attempted to call Josephine to inform her of my decision, but she was not at home. I reached her later in the evening and she didn't take my decision well. We were both in tears as I told of my plans to catch a connecting bus at 0930 the next day. We both agreed to pray about the decision and I agreed to call her early the next morning for further discussion. I spent a fitful night and didn't sleep for more than 2-3 hours. (mile 1,188.7)

DAY 107 – June 24, 1997

I got up at 0400 and walked to the 3C's Truck stop where I had my fill of the best pancakes that I had found on the trail. On my way back to the pavilion, I met *Paratrooper* heading for the truck stop; it was so dark that we hardly recognized each other as we passed. He knew of my decision to leave the trail and we were both sorry that we would not be able to continue together.

I waited at the pavilion for daylight and made my way to the Port Clinton Hotel where I would call Josephine. I was still not convinced that I should continue my journey, but after talking with Josephine, she assured me that I should continue. In fact, she seemed more upset than I did about my coming off the trail.

Mr. Breon had been watching from his house to see if I was in front of the hotel for my bus connection. I walked to his house and informed him that we had made the decision that I should continue. He was very supportive and I returned to the pavilion to announce to the others that I was still game for the trek to ME. The others were planning to head out early today and I knew that I would have to go back to Hamburg to get supplied before I could get back on the trail. I went back to Mr. Breon's house at mid-morning and found him mowing his back yard. He had mowed all but a couple of strips around his clothesline; when he saw me, he shut the mower down and I apologized for interrupting his chore. I asked if I could catch a ride later in the day when other hikers would come in and needed transportation to Hamburg. He stated that he could take me right now … I told him that I could wait and he should finish mowing his yard. He replied, "When a person has a need, that need should be met," and we left for Hamburg a few minutes later. Mr. Breon, a 72 year-old elder in his church, taught me the true meaning of servant hood. Although I didn't realize it at that time, Mr. Breon was responding to Paul's teachings in *Philippians 2:20-21*. As we rode to Hamburg he stated that he would be praying for my family and me, and I knew that this man of God would do exactly that. I purchased my supplies and gave him the sandals that I had purchased for the aborted trip home.

My water filter pump mechanism broke on June 23rd, and I had called the Sweetwater manufacturer in Boulder, CO for a replacement. The representative agreed to ship a new filter by priority mail and that it would be waiting for me when I arrived at Delaware Water Gap, PA. I made plans to head out at noon and made my way through town along the Schuykill River.

It was sweltering hot as I made the steep climb out of Port Clinton. The rocky trail was difficult and I encountered several hard climbs. I ran across a groundhog in the middle of the trail and it seemed to be burying itself in the soft terrain. As I made my way around the animal, it lurched at me. I quickly scampered out of the way, almost losing my balance in the process. Later, I would learn that another hiker had a similar encounter with the groundhog, and we suspected that it was near death, and was making final preparations for its demise.

I walked 10.3 miles before pitching my tent at The Pinnacles. I had carried a 1 lb.-8oz can of Sweet Sue Chicken and Dumplings knowing that I would consume this heavy ration on my first night out of Port Clinton. The events of the past two days had left me exhausted and I crashed at 1730. (mile 1,199.0)

DAY 108 – June 25, 1997

Today, I will reach the 1,200-mile mark. It felt good to know that I was now only 800 plus miles from my destination. Today, the heat was oppressive and the water sources were scarce. I stopped off at the Eckville Hiker's Center for fuel and snacks. I was the only one there at the time and I could not find the caretaker. *Paratrooper* had been here the day before and the hostel register indicated that he had fallen, suffering cuts, bruises, and a chipped tooth. I couldn't help feeling that he was pushing too hard in his efforts to do 100 miles per week. *Chicken Little* is out ahead of me and I hope to catch him at the next shelter; if I don't catch him there, we'll link up again at Delaware Water Gap.

The Pennsylvania rocks seem to be getting worse as I go, and the sweltering heat only adds to the misery. I can't wait to get to Delaware Water Gap where I will stay at a church hostel and get some good restaurant food. Yes! I put in early at 1330 due to he heat. The Allentown Hiking Club Shelter was a new structure, and I was alone at nightfall. Most of the PA shelters had privies and this was a luxury after a long day on the trail. The water source was a long ways down the trail, in fact, more than a mile round trip. (mile 1,212.8)

DAY 109 – June 26, 1997

I was on the trail by 0600 and walking headlong into the most unmerciful rocky terrain that I had yet to encounter. Where did Pennsylvania get all of the rocks? I walked over the Cliffs and had to pick my way with care. The blazes were difficult to locate at times, and the last thing that I wanted to do was to get off the beaten path, and then have to climb out of the deep caverns in order to get back on the white blazed trail. I had thought that the huge rocks back in southwestern Virginia were treacherous, but they paled in comparison to these in PA.

Off in the distance, I could hear the traffic sounds from the Pennsylvania Turnpike, a sullen reminder that civilization was not too far from the isolation of the trail. I made my way to the George W. Outerbridge Shelter where I tented next to a flowing spring; it sure was good to have plenty of water after the past few days of scarcity. PA was taking its toll on my boots as well as my aching feet. At day's end, I had traveled 17.9 miles; thus far, my only fond memories of PA seemed to be the small towns that I had passed through. (mile 1,230.6)

DAY 110 – June 27, 1997

I left at 0600 heading towards Slatington, PA, where I planned to get off for food and laundry. When I reached PA 248, I made my way across the bridge that spanned the Lehigh River and headed for the Maple Springs Restaurant. While eating, I met an interesting gentleman who ran a nearby aviation strip. He was an entrepreneur of sorts who had traveled extensively in the former Soviet Union, where he sold hot air balloons. He related that he had dealt with the Soviet Mafia in his transactions and told of daring encounters with the KGB. He seemed legitimate and I was intrigued by his stories.

The lady who operated the restaurant with her son agreed to secure my pack while I walked an additional two miles into the town of Slatington to do my laundry. I made my way back to the restaurant and loaded up for my walk back to the trailhead. Little did I know that one of the hardest climbs of the entire AT was just ahead.

As I continued across the Lehigh River Bridge, I could see this huge mound of boulders directly ahead and attempted to convince myself that I would surely not have to cross this obstacle. I picked up a white blaze at the end of the bridge and made a right turn ... so far, so good. I walked past a construction crew and made my way to where the road forked. I could not spot a white blaze and crossed the road to proceed on the left fork, where I desperately hoped to locate a white blaze. After walking a 100-yards or so, I knew that I was on a wild goose chase and began to backtrack to the point where I had first encountered the construction crew. I asked a flagman if he had seen any hikers coming through and if he knew where the AT picked up. He pointed to an opening in the wood line and informed me that he had seen some hikers heading there.

In a short while, I was standing at the base of that huge mound of boulders, and the white blazes were very visible. By now, it was 1030 and the weather was sunny with a brisk breeze. I surveyed this huge rock mound and took my first step toward the hardest climb that I had encountered, thus far. The first mile or so, required hand-over-hand climbing, and at times I paused to catch my breath before venturing another step across the jagged boulders. As I slowly made my way upward, I wondered how anyone with claustrophobia could make this passage. When I reached the summit, I felt a real sense of accomplishment, and gave thanks that I did not have to make the climb in bad weather. I took my pack off and looked back at the spectacular view of the Lehigh River and the town of Slatington.

I knew from my data book that water would be hard to come by; I had two full liters of water that I hoped would get me to the next shelter. By the time that I had reached the Leroy A. Smith Shelter, my water was consumed and my feet were aching from the 20-mile trek. I pitched my tent and then went in search of water down an abandoned road in front of the shelter. I walked an additional mile past two dried up springs before I reached the third spring, which was barely running. At days end, I had walked an additional two miles round trip to retrieve the precious fluid. I pitched my tent in an open area away from the shelter and needless to say, I crashed and slept well this evening. (mile 1,247.3)

DAY 111 – June 28, 1997

I was wide-awake at 0445, following a good nights sleep. *Harry-Carry*, *Bird Man*, *Mega Man*, *Ten Thumbs*, and *The Tick* had spent the night at the shelter. I had pitched my tent under some pines and for a change, the terrain was fairly level. As I fired my stove in preparation for a very early morning breakfast, I caught a reflection off my tent and stuck my head out to see what was scurrying about. I came face-to-face with a skunk that scampered off into the woods. Fortunately for me, he wasn't in a foul mood and spared me the dreaded odor.

I was on the trail by 0600 and walked until 1300, where I stopped at Kirkridge Shelter, the last shelter before Delaware Water Gap. A scout troop came in soon after I arrived and set up camp. To my utter amazement, the two adult scout leaders set their tent up inside the shelter. This was a no-no in terms of trail etiquette, as any tent will take up additional space that can be used by other hikers. It was a good thing that the other thru-hikers went ahead, or we would have had a confrontation.

We entertained ourselves for the remainder of the day by watching the hang gliders that soared directly over our shelter. They seemed so graceful in flight and I wondered where they would land in the valley below. I've always been intrigued by the thought of hang gliding ... could this be my next challenge? The mosquitoes and black flies were unmerciful; I slept with a head net for the first, and only time, while on the trail. (mile 1,260.7)

DAY 112 – June 29, 1997

I was on the trail at 0500 and made my way down the steep 6.4-mile descent that would lead me to Delaware Water Gap. I planned to stay at the Presbyterian Church of the Mountain that was established in 1854. The Reverend Karen Nickels operated this hostel especially for long-distance hikers ... boy, did I ever qualify!

I hit the pavement leading into town around 0800 and picked up my pace, as I was anxious to check in at the hostel. I then moved on to the Post Office; sure enough, my water filter replacement was awaiting me. The equipment suppliers were very prompt in replacing items for us thru-hikers, as they knew we were walking billboards for their products. As I made my way back to the church hostel, the first person that I saw was *Bird Man,* who was perched in a phone booth. I went over to where he was placing his call and gave him a high five. For some reason, I felt in a celebratory mood. The idea that Pennsylvania and the treacherous rocky terrain was about to be put behind me, seemed to give me a sense of jubilation, as it did the others. I waited my turn for the shower and pitched my tent under a spreading elm tree in back of the church parsonage. The grass had just been freshly mowed and was it ever nice to find a flat spot on which to set my tent. *Bird Man* and *Harry-Carry* had already pitched their tents in the shadow of the giant tree.

I headed for town to find the Water Gap Diner and ran into *Chicken Little,* who announced that he was moving on this afternoon. We made plans to attend the morning worship service, and I proceeded in search of the diner. I quickly scarfed down my favorite meal of the day and was served by the most efficient waitress that I have ever seen. I complemented her, and mentioned her efficiency to her boss before leaving. Upon returning to the hostel, I called Josephine to share my good fortune of making it through PA.

Chicken Little and I attended the morning church service. Afterwards, I went back into town to pick up some fruit and pastries from the local bakery. This was absolutely the best bakery that I would encounter on the trail. Delaware Water Gap tended to be a recreation area for the well-to-do residents of nearby New Jersey, and the Jags, BMW's, and Porches were out in force. I could hardly believe the speeds with which they traveled on the narrow streets of this little hamlet.

I returned to the basement area of the church hostel where it was cool. The weather had been sweltering and it felt good just to recline in an easy chair, and read from the rack that had been provided for us hikers. *Chicken Little* had left some inspirational cards that he had ordered from Maggie Sill back in Front Royal, VA. As he departed that afternoon, he embraced me and thanked me for witnessing to him on the trail. He was so sincere that I felt gratified knowing that I had made an impact on his spiritual life. He departed by mid-afternoon and this would be the last time that I would see him on the trail. Later in the day, *Paratrooper* came in ... he looked bad; he recounted how he had fallen, broken his thumb and chipped a front tooth. We were both happy to see each other and went back to the diner after he showered. I almost decided to stay another day and night at the hostel, but I liked the group that I was with and decided to move out the next day. (mile 1,267.1)

Delaware Water Gap PA	
Unionville NY	51.4 mi
Vernon NJ	64.3 mi
NY – CT Line	161.2 mi

-7-
TEARING UP THE TURNPIKE
NEW JERSEY/NEW YORK

> The states of New Jersey and New York are defined as Mid-Atlantic Lowlands, as the Hudson River is only 176 feet above sea level. These two states offered a combined total of 162-miles of AT. It was July and the rock cliffs, box car-sized boulders, and scarcity of water took its toll, as even more hikers began leaving the trail.

D AY 113 – June 30, 1997
I was up at 0500 and waited on *Paratrooper* to fall out so that we could go for breakfast; he was an early riser like me, but it took him longer to pack up for the trail due to the configuration of his pack. We departed at noon and made it to Sunfish Pond, where *Bird Man* decided to stop for a swim. I was tempted to take a dip in the pond, but decided to move on with *Paratrooper*.

We pressed on to Flatrock Road where we pitched our tents. We had walked 17.4 miles since leaving at noon and we were both exhausted. *Paratrooper* developed a nosebleed, and I was beginning to have concerns about how hard he had been pushing. By the time that we had set up camp, it was 1930. We got our water from a pump well and it really tasted of iron ... we didn't care though, as it beat having to walk in search of another water source. We both crashed after the evening meal and slept like two rocks. (mile 1,284.5)

DAY 114 – July 1, 1997
We were both up at 0500 and didn't break camp until almost 0730. The trail was rocky, but not as bad as yesterday. It felt so good to finally be out of PA, that we vowed to take New Jersey in stride. We were looking forward to getting to Branchville, NJ, where we planned to stop for some restaurant food.

We spotted a roadhouse and ordered a $4. cheeseburger; the bar waitress seemed none to happy to serve two grungy hikers, but by now, we were used to this. We ate outside on a picnic table overlooking a lake; the sun was warm and we both had difficulty in getting back to the grind. The bakery that had been highlighted in our data books was closed on Tuesdays.

We missed the shelter a Gren Anderson and had to move on to Mashipacong Shelter for our water. *Paratrooper* decided to stay in the shelter while I pitched my tent on a wooden platform. The heat was taking a toll on us, and I vowed not to do a long day tomorrow; we had knocked out 19.6 miles today. We made plans to walk to High Point State Park tomorrow for a quick shower and some food at the concession stand. A heavy fog settled in later in the evening and when I got up to go to the privy, I got lost in the fog and had a difficult time finding my way back to my tent. (mile 1,304.4)

DAY 115 – July 2, 1997

We left the shelter at 0800 and walked 5.5 miles to High Point State Park, and then another two-miles to the concession. I had two of the sorriest hamburgers that I had ever eaten ... no dressing, except catsup! Two dissatisfied hikers skipped the shower and were back of the trail by noon.

It rained off and on all the way to our next exit at Unionville, NY. On this day, we would encounter our first sustained plank walks. This area of the AT was extremely marshy and the trail maintenance crews had laid split logs to span the marshes. Little did we know that we had many more miles of walking planks before we reached Maine. We took a left when we hit the hard top road, hoping that the road would lead to Unionville. After walking for a mile or two, I heard a hammering sound up a dirt road and walked a few hundred yards until I came to a house that was being renovated. I got the attention of one of the workman and he informed me that we were on the right road to Unionville. The crew seemed somewhat taken back by the fact that we had walked all the way from Georgia and were headed to Maine.

We continued the 2-mile walk into Unionville and made our way past a picturesque church, where I stopped to take a picture. It was on to the Back Track Inn ... boy, were we ever in for a shock! The accommodations were merely a cinder block attachment to the bar that was billed as an Inn. No doubt, it had been used for a storage shed, as the shelves were still in place. We each paid the bartender $6. and spread our sleeping bags on the shelves that served as bunks. I had stayed in many a trail shelter that was better than this, but after the long walk into town, we weren't about to backtrack to the trail this evening. The shower was the absolute worst that we had ever seen; basically, it was located in an attachment built on the backside of the bar. There was no commode, thus we had to use the bathroom located in the bar that closed at midnight ... we were on our own after that. There was one redeeming grace ... the bar served up a great cheeseburger/fries plate and I must have drunk a gallon of iced tea. The bartender resembled Ted Danson of Cheers fame and he was none too friendly, as the owner had left him to tend the bar, in addition to the kitchen chores. One of the patrons gave us a loaf of raisin bread and we split it for the next day's journey.

After dinner, we settled in and laughed about our meager surroundings. We sat down on the front stoop, watched the locals frequent the bar, and tried to process the events of the day. I walked back up the main street to the town's only grocery, where I purchased milk and cakes to top off this memorable day. (mile 1,318.8)

DAY 116 – Checking out of the Back Track Inn.

DAY 116 – July 3, 1997

I was up before *Paratrooper* and walked the three blocks to the grocery store to get our morning coffee; freshly brewed coffee was such a treat after our usual instant coffee on the trail. We packed up and went to breakfast at Side Road Kitchen, a Mom & Pop operation, located in a former residence. We were on our way out of town by 0800 and enjoyed the walk through this picturesque little town that time had forgotten.

Today's 17.6-mile walk to Vernon, NJ would take us through the Wallkill River Valley known for its rich, black, loamy soil. We got our water from a hand pump near Pochuck Mountain Shelter and moved on. Several of the hikers planned to get off at County Road 565 for an overnight stay at the Apple Valley Inn. A couple from Alabama maintained accommodations for five thru-hikers at their upscale establishment. Tomorrow would be the 4th of July, and we knew that we did not stand a chance at getting a room without reservations. With this in mind, we moved full steam ahead to Vernon. We walked through miles of rolling farmland before reaching County Road 517. We thought that we had reached NJ 94 and turned left in search of Heaven Hill Farm, where we hoped to pick up a snack. After a short "goose chase," we decided to turn back and thumb a ride into Vernon. The sun was really beaming down and we were both disgusted at having walked an extra mile or two for naught.

After a while, we caught a ride in the back of a pickup and the driver deposited us at our destination, the Vernon Volunteer Fire Department Pavilion. We were the only two hikers to stay at the pavilion. A restroom was open and we cold washed our clothes in the lavatory and strung a line near the pavilion. We shopped a nearby A&P grocery and settled in for the evening. The Pavilion was quite large and held approximately 20-25 picnic tables under the sprawling roof. We perched our sleeping bags on top of two of the tables that would serve as our bed for the night. We jokingly remarked that this was better accommodation than we had back in Unionville, and we didn't have to pay $6. to spend the night. Earlier today, the volunteer firemen held a meeting under the pavilion to discuss their game plan for tomorrow's 4th of July parade. After the meeting broke, I struck up a conversation with Big John, a volunteer, who offered us a ride back to the trailhead in the morning. (mile 1,331.0)

DAY 117 – July 4, 1997
We walked to a bagel shop, had a nice breakfast and returned to the pavilion to await Big John; he kept his promise to be there at 0800. We thanked him for the ride and headed north over some good terrain that was interspersed with a few ups and downs. This good terrain would soon end, as we crossed in to New York. Before long, we encountered hand-over-hand cliff climbing. Our thigh muscles were aching, and we were consuming water at a record pace. The sun was unmerciful, as we scrambled over one cliff after another. We were without water by mid-afternoon, and quenched our thirst by eating blueberries that dotted the trail.

We arrived at Wildcat Shelter just before 1900 and got our water from a hand pump well. We were getting used to the rusty looking, iron laden water. This 4th of July would be one that we would long remember. There would be no hotdogs, hamburgers, sodas, or firecrackers for us this day. The scorching heat, being reflected from the granite faced cliffs, took its toll on our feet and aching leg muscles. We decided not to pitch our tents and crashed early; I slept well and didn't wake up until 0445 the next morning. (mile 1,348.8)

DAY 118 – July 5, 1997

We departed Wildcat Shelter at 0700, after having been the only occupants in the shelter last night. Our trail data book indicated more of the same for today's walk. As we moved forward, I could not help but recall the rugged Pennsylvania trail with all of its rocky pitfalls. Given the option, I still preferred the NY terrain, and attempted to convince myself that the worst was behind me. Just before we arrived at NY 17, I twisted my left knee on a steep downhill portion of the trail. I led off with my left foot, planting it on a small tree stump that protruded from the side of the trail. The stump gave way as I placed my full weight on it, thus causing my leg to twist. I knew immediately what I had done, but kept moving, as I knew that my leg would become stiff if I took a break. *Paratrooper* planned to get off the trail again, for a visit with a daughter in New York. He was looking forward to the visit, but planned to get back on the trail by Sunday afternoon, so that he could catch up with me. I planned to move on to Island Pond Outlet, which was only 1.7 miles from NY 17.

When I arrived at the pond, there were several people there; most of them had walked in for a picnic or to just lounge around the pond. This would be my first time to filter water from a pond and I didn't exactly relish the idea. My filter would purify the water, but the fluid still came from a warm body of non-flowing water. I boiled the water just to make sure that I didn't pick up a bug that might cause dysentery. It was here that I met a day hiker by the name of Richard D'Alessandro, who gave me a bottle of tea that he had carried in to the pond. I was very appreciative of the drink and even though it was warm, it sure beat drinking warm pond water.

This was a no-camping area, so I decided to take my chances by moving up the AT and circling around to the other side of the pond. I pitched my tent near a large rock formation that hid it from view of the main access road leading to the pond. I spent a great afternoon sunning by the pond, where I rinsed my sweat soaked tee shirts and hung them on some limbs. The gash on my leg was healing nicely and I could see that the Crazy Glue had done its intended job. I bided my time by writing some postcards and catching up on my log notes. I was behind on my notes by at least two days, due to the rigors of the trail and utter exhaustion at day's end. Just before my evening meal, I took a dip in the pond just to say that I had been for a swim. Recently, I had passed up too many good swimming holes and vowed not to continue this pattern. (mile 1,359.4)

DAY 119 – July 6, 1997

I broke camp and was back on the trail by 0600. It was a great day for walking and I decided to move on for another four miles, where I would walk into Harriman State Park, the second largest park in New York. I shaved at the restroom facility, called home, and had a coke from the visitor's center. I left the park around 0900 with two full liters of water heading to West Mountain Shelter. It was a clear day and by noon the temperature was in the low 90's. I filtered three more liters from a small stream after passing Fingerboard Shelter, and I had good intentions of making it to West Mountain Shelter. The extra weight of the water and the blazing heat caused me to put up approximately one-half mile short of my planned destination.

I tented on a plateau where I had plenty of sunlight to air my sleeping bag. The afternoon sun, accompanied by a slight breeze, was a welcome venue. I was off the trail by some 100 yards, and hung my food just in case there might be bears in the area. I really felt alone this evening and relished the thought that *Paratrooper* would rejoin me in a few days. My next stop would be the Graymoor Friary, run by Franciscan Friars of the Atonement, near Bear Mountain, NY. (mile 1,363.2)

DAY 120 – July 7, 1997

I broke camp at 0600 and walked five miles to Bear Mountain State Park, where I had a continental breakfast at the Inn. The AT would take me right through the Trailside Museum and Zoo. I didn't pay much attention to the featured nature exhibits, as the walk from Georgia to New York had exposed me to all of the nature that I could take for this lifetime. I did stop at the statue of Walt Whitman for a photo opportunity.

As I exited the zoo, I made a sharp right turn and stared at the Bear Mountain Bridge that spanned the Hudson River. A giant American Flag swaggered in the breeze high above the bridge, and I was reminded that West Point was not too far from here. The skies were beginning to darken and I knew that I would not make it to Graymoor Friary without a good drenching. After crossing the bridge, I picked up my pace until I came to a service station where I stopped for a soda and some snacks. I could see the storm front moving in and asked the operator if I could bring my pack inside to wait out the storm. He was none too friendly, but indicated that it would be all right.

After the rains slowed, I decided to move on to the Friary; I arrived at Graymoor around 1330 and had to wait until 1600 to check in. I made myself comfortable in the vestibule and took off my boots, a requirement for all hikers who enter the complex. I shaved and found my way to the soda and snack machines. At precisely 1600, a friar dressed in full cloak, came to greet me and asked if any other hikers were with me. We waited for a few minutes for others to arrive and when no one showed, he guided me to my quarters located in the original wing of the friary. I had my pick of several small, private rooms equipped with a bunk and a washbasin. Hot showers, washer and dryer were located down the hallway in a common use area. The friar left to go back to the main complex to await the other hikers.

Much to my surprise, *Paratrooper* arrived along with several other hikers. I was really glad to se him, as I thought that he would be at least a full day behind me. He had his sights on averaging 17 milers per day, or 100 miles per week. He's a tough old bird and when he makes up his mind to do something, he does it! His four years in the Marine Corps surely left a mark on him. I guess that it why we are so compatible.

We all headed for the evening meal that was served in the main cafeteria, where a special table had been reserved for thru-hikers. The Graymoor Friary was renowned for the quantity of food that they served. You should have seen us famished hikers chowing down on a spaghetti supper. We cleaned everything in sight and left with full stomachs. Some were already talking about the breakfast that would be served at 0730 in the morning. I walked around the grounds and took several photos. This would surely be one of my most unusual experiences on the AT. I packed my clean clothing and made ready for sleeping on a real bed tonight. (mile 1,383.4)

I could truthfully say that I was not sorry to have put New York and New Jersey behind me. The sweltering hot temperatures and the scarcity of water added to the discomfort of the rock-laden trail. As I was about to enter the state of Connecticut, I knew that my greatest challenges were yet to come.

NY-CT Line

Kent CT	11.6 mi
Sheffield MA	67.0 mi
MA-VT Line	141.7 mi
Manchester Center VT	196.5 mi
Hanover NH	289.3 mi

CLIMB EVERY MOUNTAIN
CONNECTICUT/MASSACHUSETTS/VERMONT

DAY 121 – July 8, 1997
We left Graymoor Friary at 0830; the youngsters got out ahead and *Harry-Carry*, *Paratrooper*, and I followed. When we arrived at Dennytown Road, the water source that was identified in our data books was not available, as the pump was out of order. We took a break and lamented the fact that our water sources would be scarce for the better part of this day. I ended up filtering water from a dingy creek, and hoped that this would do me until we could get to Clarence Fahnestock State Park.

We continued on the trail that led to a view of Canopus Lake, located in the park. *Harry-Carry* had been through this section of the trail on several occasions and knew of a steep trail that led to the concession area on the lake. The other hikers decided to go for a cheeseburger and soda; I didn't think it worthwhile, and stayed behind to keep an eye on their gear. The weather was beginning to turn bad ... the rain was light at first, and then it became apparent that a major storm was brewing.

Paratrooper came back to indicate that he and *Harry-Carry* were going to stay in the park campground. I decided to join them and we made our way back down the steep slope leading to the campground. The other hikers had decided to move on to the next shelter. We walked to the campground and pitched our tents. The Rangers usually allowed thru-hikers to stay free of charge and no one came around to collect. We had a hot shower and plenty of good water for a change. The storm front blew through and we learned the next day that the others had encountered severe weather, to include heavy rain, lightening, and hail. This had been a short day, as we only covered 13.1 miles. (mile 1,395.2)

DAY 122 – July 9, 1997
The three of us departed Farnsworth State Park at 0730 and headed towards Morgan Stewart Shelter. The weather was hot and muggy with several steep climbs. We stopped at a deli that was .4 mile off the trail ... had a Rubin sandwich, half-gallon of ice cream, a full liter of coke, Famous Amos cookies, and carried out a meatball sandwich ... not a bad lunch. These off-trail delis were beginning to be habit forming, and I was concentrating more on obtaining food than I was in moving ahead to Mt. Katahdin. If I hadn't been traveling in

the company of *Harry-Carry*, I probably would not have known of these off-trail eateries; I wasn't complaining though.

I was bolstered with food and got out ahead of the others, as I wanted desperately to reach the next shelter before the storm hit. Despite my good efforts, the storm hit when I was about one mile short of Morgan Stewart Shelter. When I arrived, two other hikers were settled in. *Paratrooper* and *Harry-Carry* came in 30 minutes later. We were all soaked to the bone; the storm front blew over and by 1700. I laced my rice dinner with some of the meatballs that I had carried from the deli ... talk about good ... I needed some reward for having been drenched today. (mile 1,410.8)

DAY 123 – July 10, 1997

I left the shelter around 0730 heading for Telephone Pioneers Shelter. It was hot and muggy and the terrain varied from open farmland, to bogs, to rugged climbs. All in all, this was a tough day. Just before reaching a rail crossing known as the Appalachian Trail Station, I caught up with *Bird Man* and *Grump.* As I crossed NY 52, I spotted a trailer concession that was pulled over at a roadside park. You guessed correctly; I stopped for two hot dogs and a soda. The lady running the concession invited me to sit down in one of the lawn chairs next to the trailer ... it sure felt strange not to set on the ground while eating.

When I crossed County Road 20, I walked under the Dover Oak, the largest oak tree on the AT. *Bird Man* and I took each other's picture under the giant tree. I arrived at Wiley Shelter an hour and a half ahead of *Paratrooper* and *Harry-Carry*. I pitched my tent and crashed ... I was experiencing diarrhea ... most likely the meatballs and hot-dogs with onions ... no wonder! *Harry-Carry* suggested that I eat some cottage cheese when we arrive in Kent, CT. (mile 1,418.2)

DAY 124 – July 11, 1997

I left camp at 0630 heading for Kent, CT. It sure would be good to put another state behind me; when I cross into CT ... nine down and five to go! The trail into CT was great for a while. I followed Ten Mile River for a short distance, and then the trail cut back into New York. I would encounter lots of steep climbs before the trail veered back into CT.

I hit the hard top at CT 341 and headed into Kent. This upscale New England village is fondly referred to by trail people as "Yuppieville." The surrounding area counts as residents such luminaries as Henry Kissinger, Joyce Brothers, Kevin Bacon, and Oscar de la Renta. I made my way past the Kent School for Boys and headed for the town's main street. It was not yet 1330, as I headed towards the Fife & Drum Inn, where I hoped to find lodging.

As I made my way through town, I heard someone shout, "Hey, *Easy Strider!*" It was none other than *The Spice Girls,* and *Sir Lancelot.* I could hardly believe my ears, as I never expected to catch my former trail chums after coming off the trail for eight days during Chris' surgery. We greeted each other like long lost brothers and sisters. I explained that I had taken on a new trail name, *Reveille,* upon returning to the trail following our son's surgery. The three of them planned to depart Kent today. I informed them of my plans to stay the night, and we rejoiced in knowing that we would be able to walk the rest of the way in close proximity.

I made my way to the Fife & Drum Inn and luckily acquired the last available room. I checked in and left word with the clerk that *Paratroope*r, and another hiker would be sharing the room. I did my laundry, shopped for groceries, and just soaked up the atmosphere of this quaint little New England village. I decided to eat at the restaurant located at the Inn and this would teach me a lesson about New England customs. I had a great pork loin dinner and asked the waitress for refills on my iced tea. Much to my surprise, my tea tab was $4., almost as much as my main course dinner. Oh well, I chalked this up to experience, and made note that I was well above the Mason Dixon Line. The never-empty vessels of coffee and tea were a thing of the past. Our room was small, but very clean and we ordered a rollaway bed, so as to accommodate the three of us. (mile 1,439.9)

DAY 125 – July 11, 1997

Paratrooper and I departed Kent around 1130; *Harry-Carry* left earlier, and we would never see him again. He was a seasoned thru-hiker, and he probably decided that he was walking too slowly with the pace that we had been setting. Most thru-hikers hold dearly to the concept of, "hiking your own hike." Since we were getting such a late start, we only planned to do 12.5 miles to Silver Hill Campsite.

We encountered several steep climbs and walked for miles along a beautiful, raging river that was popular for white water canoeing. The heavy rains had caused the river to surge, and we did not see anyone on the river. Our pack weight was well over 50 lb., and we both struggled on the climbs. We met a trail maintenance volunteer on the river and he gave us an orange; he was headed to Silver Hill Campsite and we followed him for a while. We were within 1.1 miles of the campsite around 1630 and due to fatigue, we overshot the trail sign leading to the campsite.

By now, we had traversed a very steep portion of the trail and neither of us felt the urge to back track to the campsite. We came to CT 4 and walked approximately 500 yards before coming to a river. With plenty of available water, we decided to find a tent site in the pine forest that bordered CT4. We were exhausted at day's end ... the mosquitoes were ferocious ... we ate and crashed for the night. (mile 1,451.4)

DAY 126 – July 12, 1997

I left camp at 0630 and *Paratrooper* followed about an hour later. I walked for an hour before coming to a pretty overlook, where I stopped to read from *Our Daily Bread*. I was beginning to feel the need for some space and realized that I had been walking *Paratrooper's* walk, rather than mine. I felt energized today and planned to set down after a short 12.5 miles to Belter Campsite. The trail was mostly rolling with only a few steep climbs ... the easiest walk in some time. I arrived at the campsite at 1400, and *Paratrooper* came in at 1530. He was bushed and I got his water for him while he pitched his tent; we help each other any way that we can. We calculated that we were less than 700 miles from Mt. Katahdin and less than 20 miles from the MA State line. (mile 1,463.6)

DAY 127 – July 14, 1997

We left early and the morning air was already humid. The trail was not too difficult today, but the humidity took its toll; we decided to pack it in at Riga Lean-to. We located a spring next to the trail and were thankful that we didn't have to go in search of water.

Trigger, *Henny-Penny* and *Dear Heart* came in later. I had not seen the later two since Mt. Rogers Ranger Headquarters, back in Virginia. They had skipped all of PA, NJ, and NY; they caught a bus to Kent, CT and were back on the trail. We settled in and fought the mosquitoes all evening ... a warm breeze prevailed ... we knew that thundershowers were in the forecast for tomorrow. (mile 1,477.5)

DAY 128 – Crossing into MA.

DAY 128 – July 15, 1997

I left camp at 0640 and *Paratrooper* followed. Talk about humidity ... we were soaking wet by 1030. Bear Mountain was our first 2,000-footer since PA; then there was Race Mountain, followed by Mt. Everett. The views would have been spectacular save for the heavy smog that had settled in the valleys below. By early afternoon, I knew that I wasn't going beyond Glen Brook Shelter. *Paratrooper* seemed to want to do more mileage, but I reasoned that he could go ahead if he so desired. I pitched my tent and was more than glad to put this hard day behind me. (mile 1,487.4)

DAY 129 – July 16, 1997

We left at 0640 and faced another hot, humid day. We walked to MA 41 and headed for the 1.2-mile walk into the town of South Egremont, where we hoped to get a good breakfast. I called home and met a local at a phone booth who offered us a ride back to the trailhead. We thanked him for the lift and headed northward to US 7. After walking a short distance, we spotted a vegetable market where we stopped for snacks. I purchased three ears of corn for my evening meal and the clerk shucked the corn for me ... no need in carrying unnecessary weight. We soon came upon a monument commemorating the last battle of Shays Rebellion, February 27, 1787.

To this point, the day had been very pleasant, however the last 9.9 miles to Tom Leonard Shelter was something else ... one stiff climb after another ... I thought that we would never get there! On several occasions, we were fooled by the huge granite outcroppings along the trail. We both swore that we could see the shelter up ahead, only to discover that the shadows were playing tricks. When we did arrive, there was not a suitable area to pitch our tents, so we decided to stay in the shelter; we were alone except for the ever-present mosquitoes. A south-bounder came in during the wee hours of the morning and made his way over a mound of rocks, where he settled in for the night. *Paratrooper* heard him come in and marveled at the fact that he didn't use a flashlight to find his way. The next morning we spoke with him and learned that he had hiked this section of the trail before, thus explaining how he found his way into the campsite. (mile 1,501.6)

DAY 130 – July 17, 1997

We left a 0645 ... fairly good trail ... not too many climbs until the last two miles. Water was available most of the way. We both decided that we were not consuming enough water, as the heat and humidity was sapping our strength. I passed up two great swimming holes today ... again; I'm allowing *Paratrooper* to influence me in his effort to meet his goal of 100 miles per week. He admits that the trail has lost its glamour for him since PA and NY. I made up my mind to stop and smell the roses along the way, as this will be the only time that I would experience the entire AT. We are such good friends, that I don't want to offend him, but he has the option to move ahead if I lag behind for a few dips. We found some raspberries along the trail and consumed our fair share before pushing on beyond Webster Road; we pitched our tents beside a small creek. We planned to get off the trail at US 20 tomorrow and hitch a ride to Lee, MA. (mile 1,518.3)

DAY 131 – July 18, 1997

We walked past the trail leading to Upper Goose Pond Cabin, a showcase facility for thru-hikers. Most of our fellow hikers had planned to stop over here and partake of the glacial pond; our timing was off, or we would have done the same. I went ahead and arrived at US 20 before 0930. I proceeded to the Gaslight Motor Lodge, where I lucked out and got the last room that was available. The lady was very nice and let us have the room for $60. She could have charged more, as a craft fair was taking place in nearby Lee, MA.

Paratrooper came in about an hour later and by that time, I had showered and begun to sort my dirty clothes for laundry. We had twin beds, black & white TV, and no AC. Even at this, we were happy to have these creature comforts for the evening. We hired a taxi and went into Lee where we ate at Joe's Diner, which had been portrayed in one of Norman Rockwell's paintings. The painting of the *"Cop and the Runaway Boy,"* was staged at Joe's; he was the waiter behind the counter, and he still runs the establishment. It was here that we had some of the best sandwiches that we had eaten on the trail. I stopped in at McCalken Drug Store, where they operate an old-fashioned fountain bar. I had a 5-cent cup of coffee and a hot fudge sundae for $2.; the soda fountain continues to offer delicacies at 1940 prices. This was really a neat town with a lot of interesting history behind it.

We did our laundry and caught a taxi back to the motel. That afternoon, I went for a swim in the lake behind the motel, while *Paratrooper* went to a roadside restaurant with *The Spice Girls*, who stayed in a room next to ours. I really enjoyed and needed the leisure time off. I felt totally relaxed, as I wrote letters to folks back home. The weather was clearing and the forecast was for cooler weather this evening. *Paratrooper's* sister and brother-in-law were to meet him tomorrow, as they were vacationing in the area in their motor home. We planned to go back into Lee tomorrow. (mile 1,524.4)

DAY 132 – July 19, 1997
Paratrooper's family came by early and took us to Joe's Dinner for breakfast. Later, we walked around town and visited the craft fair in the town square. I bought Josephine a ladybug refrigerator magnet and just enjoyed the atmosphere of this little New England town. I ran into a policeman who gave me a rundown on some of the town's history. I really enjoyed *Paratrooper's* family and became aware of my longing to be with my own family.

We made our way back to the motel where we ran into *Sir Lancelot, Peanut Butter, Grump,* and *The Spice Girls*; they were making plans to slack the next section of the trail. As for us two old fuddy-duddies, we would have none of that … hard core, all the way! We left the motel around 1100; the weather was brisk with a slight breeze and low humidity … we certainly were overdue for some decent weather. We had a great 16-mile walk and tented at Kay Wood Lean-to around 1800. (mile 1,540.3)

DAY 133 – July 20, 1997
I left Kay Wood Lean-to at 0715. *Paratrooper* was slower in getting out this morning, so I went ahead. I arrived in Dalton around 0900 and stopped at a hole-in-the-wall restaurant, where *Sir Lancelot, The Spice Girls*, and others were already chowing down. *Paratrooper* came in and we had breakfast together, while we enjoyed the company of the others.

After a phone call to the home front, we left Dalton heading for our next stop at Cheshire, MA. We had a devil of a time finding the white blazed trail that would lead us out of town. *Sir Lancelot* caught up and walked with us the remainder of the day; it seemed like old times having him in the group. We arrived at St. Mary of the Assumption Catholic Church hostel around 1430, and found our sleeping spaces in a large auditorium. The main restaurant in town was closed for their vacation period, thus we ended up at a family run deli that served great hoagie sandwiches. I never cease to be amazed at these quaint little New England villages. I killed some time by walking the main street, and dropped in at the only Baptist Church in town. I met the pastor and picked up some literature for the trail. I looked forward to tomorrow, as we would be only one day shy of crossing into Vermont. (mile 1,552.6)

DAY 134 – July 21, 1997
Today, everyone left ahead of me, and for some reason, I seemed to be in no hurry to get out of town. I waited for the Post Office to open and picked up the mail drop that Josephine had sent me. I departed town around 1000 and it sprinkled most of the day, as I made my way up Mt. Greylock, the highest point in MA at 3,500 feet. *Paratrooper* and the others were at Bascomb Lodge when I arrived. I ordered a cheeseburger and soda and enjoyed the warmth of the lodge. *Sir Lancelot* and some of the others were doing a work-for-stay at the lodge. This meant that they would have overnight lodging, at no cost, for helping out with various chores at the lodge; sort of like KP duty in the Army.

Paratrooper and I left the lodge in a slight drizzle and a heavy shroud of fog. We walked a very slippery trail for 11.2 miles to Wilbur Clearing Lean-to. I was the first in, and one other person was in the shelter when I arrived. He was carrying a blue pack and had the start of a full beard ... about 45 years of age with average build ... he was spread out and appeared to be reading. I asked him for directions to the water source and he pointed and mumbled something that I did not understand. I immediately got bad vibes from this person and set out on my own to find the water. By the time that I had returned from filtering my water, *Paratrooper* had arrived and asked if this person had seen me. According to *Paratrooper*, the man responded in a snappy manner. When *Paratrooper* attempted to apologize for disturbing him, the man responded my snapping, "Don't worry about it!" We both pitched our tents away from the shelter and decided that this man was "bad news." Some hikers did come in and stayed in the shelter without difficulty. This would mark the first, and only time that I would encounter anyone on the trail that gave off such anti-social vibes. We never saw this individual on the trail after this encounter and surmised that he was running from something ... perhaps, himself. Only 7.1 miles tomorrow and we will cross into Vermont. (1,563.7)

The AT merges with "The Long Trail" at the Vermont-Massachusetts state line; it is here the two trails become one for the next 104 miles. At Main Junction, just north of Sherburne Pass, the AT rambles eastward where it terminates at Mt. Katahdin; "The Long Trail" continues northward for another 165 miles before crossing into Canada. Built between 1910 and 1930, "The Long Trail" is the oldest long-distance trail in the United States and served as the inspiration for the Appalachian Trail.

DAY 135 – July 22, 1997

I broke camp at 0700 and *Paratrooper* followed soon after. I walked three miles to MA 2 State Road and as I crossed the road, a vehicle turned the corner to my right. I heard a familiar voice shout, "Hey, *"Reveille"* ... it was none other than *Ginger*, the other half of *The Spice Girls*. After the long dry spell from VA to CT, we were now crossing paths every day or so. We walked the next 12 miles together as we were all headed to Congdon Camp Lean-to. About a half mile from the shelter, I decided to stop at a campsite next to a small stream, while *The Spice Girls* pushed on to the shelter. *Paratrooper* came in a short while later and pitched his tent next to mine ... what a peaceful setting. We made plans to do a leisurely 14 miles tomorrow ... today, we crossed the Vermont State line ... ten down and only four to go! (mile 1,580.9)

DAY 136 – July 23, 1997

I left camp at 0615 and walked up Harmon Hill where I stood in awe, as I looked out at Bennington, VT. I recalled that Josephine and I had visited here last October. I took a picture of the distant Bennington Monument that looked like a matchstick in the distance. I was reminded that my paternal grandfather, five times removed, had bought in the Battle of Bennington in 1777.

The weather looked threatening, and it was cold enough for long pants and my thermal top. The terrain was mostly rolling with a few steep climbs, and plenty of roots and rocks. It would turn out to be a long, arduous 14-mile day. My feet hurt, especially my left heel where my innersole had given away. I had called the boot manufacturer and a representative had agreed to send me a pair of replacement boots in Manchester Center. One good thing about being a thru-hiker was that we were walking billboards for trail outfitters. I arrived at Goddard Shelter around 1400 and found a fairly nice tent site. *Paratrooper* came in around 1630 and suffered another nosebleed; I continue to worry that he is pushing too hard. I'm thinking of cutting my mileage tomorrow if the trail stays this tough. (mile 1,595.3)

DAY 137 – July 24, 1997

As I left Goddard Shelter at 0612, the weather looked threatening ... cold enough for long pants and shirt for the first few miles. It never took long for one's body heat to reach a point that required the gradual removal of outerwear. I planned to do a short mileage day and put up near a creek just beyond Kelly Stroud Road. I rinsed some clothes in a stream. The sun never came out, so I'll hang them on my pack and let the wind dry them tomorrow ... that is, if it's not raining.

My tent site was nestled in a clump of trees and after a while, I spotted *Paratrooper* coming up the trail; he walked past without seeing me. I hollered at him and he stopped to chat awhile before he moved on to Stratton Pond Shelter. I'll face the dreaded Stratton Mountain climb in the morning. It felt good just to lie in my tent and write some letters. My plans called for me to be in Manchester Center Saturday morning in time to pick up my new boots. I'm considering staying two nights at the church hostel. Some of the hikers took a blue blazed trail to Stratton Pond Shelter ... I'm still dedicated to following the white blazes. (mile 1,604.4)

DAY 138 – July 25, 1997

I was up and on the trail by 0615. I left my hand towel hanging in a tree ... sure will miss that. It turned out to be a beautiful, autumn-like day. I had planned to camp on the AT about three miles from the highway leading to Manchester Center, but decided to move on when I reached the shelter at 1330.

I hitched a ride with a nice lady who was driving a Jeep Cherokee. She and her husband were backpackers and she often gave rides to hikers who were heading into town. She dropped me off at the Post Office where the postal clerk took my picture for their trail register. I saw that *Bird Man* had been there already, and I knew that he had taken a blue blazed trail in order to be out ahead of me. Much to my disappointment, my boots were not there. However, I did have a letter from the manufacturer that instructed me to go to the Mountain Goat Outfitters to pick up my new boots.

I made my way to the Episcopal Church hostel that was literally overflowing with hikers. I wasn't bothered in the least, as all I wanted was a hot shower. I pitched my tent directly behind the church, only to learn that *The Spice Girls* were pitched next to me. *Paratrooper* had arrived earlier in the day and had secured a floor space in the hiker hostel. I ate at McDonalds while my laundry cycled. I planned to pick up my replacement boots tomorrow. The evening was topped off with a pint of B&J ice cream, and I went to bed with a smile on my face. (mile 1,624.8)

DAY 139 – July 26, 1997

Paratrooper and I ate breakfast at a bakery, and I bought several kinds of pastry to carry back to the trail. He had talked me into getting back on the trail, and I really didn't need to stay another day just to pick up my boots. I miscalculated the time that the outfitter would open; they didn't open until 1100. By the time that I had gotten my new boots and walked back to the hostel, *Paratrooper* had secured us a ride back to the trailhead with a lady who attended the Episcopal Church. She was an impatient type and let us know that she wasn't happy about being delayed. I reluctantly asked if she would stop by the Post Office so that I could mail a package home. She did, and dropped us off at the trailhead at noon.

We began our 12-mile walk to Griffith Lake Campsite where we tented. We were now on the portion of the AT where we would be charged a fee of $5. to camp in the rigidly controlled campsites. By the time that we arrived, all of the tent platforms had been taken, and the caretaker directed us to an overflow area next to a lake. The mosquitoes were fierce and it was all that we could do to prepare our food outside the tent. We turned in a 1900 and were thankful to escape the pests. (mile 1,635.2)

DAY 140 – July 27, 1997

I left camp at 0615 and walked on to Barker Peak, where I sat down to have devotions on this Sunday morning. I passed some campers and their dog that had a bandana tied around his neck; he barked as I approached and his master soon brought him under voice control. I moved on to Lost Pond Lake, where I took my third dip on the AT. The water was sort of murky when I stirred the bottom silt, but it was wet and that was all that mattered. I set my camera on automatic and recorded the even.

I continued on until I arrived at Greenwald Shelter at 1400. *Paratrooper* came in later and decided to move on for another four miles in order to get his 17-mile average. I pitched my tent away from the shelter and prepared an early evening meal. It was here that I met *Doughboy*, a young southbound thru-hiker from Georgia. He turned out to be quite a character; he often walked the trail in sandals and prided himself in doing 24-mile days. He was among the first south-bounders that I would encounter on the way to Maine.

Rusty Roof, a north-bounder, from Alabama, soon joined me. We talked Southeastern Conference football and I kidded him about how the Tennessee Volunteers were going to beat Auburn in 1998. He was a serious type who had no use for "blue blazers," as he felt that they were cheating on the AT. (mile 1,649.1)

DAY 141 – July 28, 1997

I left camp at 0618 for Governor Clement Shelter. Around 0830, I came to a roaring river with cascades and deep holes … this was too much … I could not possibly walk past such a temptation. I didn't dare leave my pack unattended on the bluff that overlooked the river. I slowly made my way down the steep embankment, using roots and branches to support my descent. It was a risky venture, but entirely worth the effort. I found a great spot where I slid into the water to the left of a huge boulder. I was in water up to my neck and if the water had not been so cold, I could have sworn that I was in a whirlpool bath. I didn't stay in the water for long, as it was too cold. Up ahead, a man was dredging for something; he would throw a bucket attached to a rope and dredge sand and gravel. I surmised that he was prospecting for gold or some precious mineral. I waved and he acknowledged my presence.

It was now time to retrace my footsteps and make my way out of this canyon. Climbing out was a lot harder than the descent and I was relieved when I reached the top. I made my way back to the trail and walked across a bridge that spanned the river canyon. This would mark the second day in a row that I had been in the water. I walked most of the afternoon in the rain, but it sort of felt good. When I reached the shelter, I pitched my tent near a creek. Today, I am less than 500 miles from my destination. (mile 1,664.1)

DAY 142 – July 29, 1997

I departed camp at 0630 and walked uphill for two solid hours. I met *Cycle Woman* and *Sun-Brite* on the trail today. *Cycle Woman's* hiking partner had left the trail back in PA after contracting Lyme disease. They set a fast pace and walked ahead of me. I found a good spring just before the next shelter and replenished my water for the ten-mile walk to the Inn at Killington. The walk to the Inn was difficult at times, and there were several day hikers on the trail this day. Some hikers ahead of me encountered two day hikers walking with three dogs. One of the dogs was not on a leash, and it attempted to attack one of the hikers. When I arrived on the scene, the hiker was threatening the dog if the owner did not get the animal under control. This was the only threatening situation brought about by dogs that I encountered on the entire trail.

I proceeded to the Inn and had an average cheeseburger for $5.95 in the Irish Pub; some of the hikers stayed at the Inn to enjoy the bar atmosphere. I dried my tent on a nearby picnic table and moved on around 1300. I had to remind myself that I needed to make sure that I was now heading eastward on the AT. The last thing that I needed was to continue on the Long Trail, heading for Canada! I walked 2.2 miles to Mountain Meadows Lodge, where I lucked out and settled into the only room reserved for thru-hikers; the room had a double bed, stacked twin bunks, and a private bath. I selfishly hoped that no other hikers would come in for the night; they didn't, and I ended up with private accommodations.

I took a canoe trip on the lake, but the wind was so strong that it blew me back to the shore. The $26 lodging fee included breakfast the next morning, and that was when I met a nice couple from Indiana. Jack and Whitney Morrell were vacationing at the lodge and they invited me to have breakfast at their table. This setting was so beautiful that I actually felt guilty staying here without Josephine. I sent her a post card of the lodge and wished that she could have been here to enjoy the experience with me. (mile 1,676)

DAY 143 – July 30, 1997

What a great stay at Mountain Meadows Lodge. I had a great breakfast with the Hoosier couple that I met yesterday, and was ready to hit the trail at 1000. My destination for this day encompassed 15.1 miles to Wintturi Shelter. This would prove to be my toughest day in a long time … I thought the climbs would never end. I arrived at the shelter after 1800; I was dog-tired … pitched my tent, filtered water, and made supper. I really felt exhausted after all the climbs today.

Today, I had met several south-bounders who had started at Mt. Katahdin, and they had nothing but good things to say about the remaining trail in NH and ME. As I bedded down for the evening, I checked my schedule and made plans to resupply at White River, tomorrow. I am growing anxious to reach Mt. Katahdin. (mile 1,691.0)

DAY 144 – July 31, 1997

Today was truly a beautiful day … about three in a row, now. Today, I met a southbound section hiker from Knoxville, TN; his name was *Bobcat* and he was hiking with a buddy from Huntsville, AL. When his buddy saw my Tennessee tee shirt logo, he told me that a big Tennessee Volunteer fan would be coming down the trail in a few minutes. I could see him coming in the distance and made ready to greet him with a "Go Big Orange!" *Bobcat* returned the greeting and we talked about the upcoming football season. He felt sure that the football VOLS stood a good chance at a national championship.

When I arrived at Thistle Hill Shelter, it was only 1400 and the sunlight seemed to radiate all around. I went down a winding trail to get my water from a spring and made my way back to the shelter, where I made up my mind that I would go no further. I pitched my tent and just lounged around in the min-afternoon sun. Later, I prepared a chili dinner around 1500; my evening snack consisted of oatmeal and granola, as I was out of cookies and sweets ... had to save my two Snicker bars for tomorrow's journey into Hanover.

The shelter's unusual privy is featured in the February 1987 issue of *National Geographic*; the Vermont trail maintenance crews seemed to have a knack for designing unusual outhouses. As I studied my trail data book for the details of tomorrow's journey, it suddenly donned on me that today was my brother Max's birthday ... Happy Birthday, little brother! (mile 1,703.1)

DAY 145 – August 1, 1997

Today, I would put the State of Vermont behind me ... twelve down and two to go! As I left camp by myself at 0545, I looked forward to the 14.5-mile walk to Hanover, New Hampshire. I was excited about the prospects of staying on the Dartmouth College campus. The day was clear and I walked for several miles through rolling evergreen forests. The pine needles that covered the trail seemed to cushion my footsteps, as I hurried my pace towards Hanover.

At mid-morning, I was filtering water from a small stream when I heard someone coming in my direction. It turned out to be a 23 year-old recent graduate of Dartmouth, named Christi. She was out for a walk and stopped to talk with me. She related that she planned to hike the AT next year and would be interested in hearing about some of my experiences. I told her that I was heading for Hanover and she stated that she would walk with me, if I didn't mind. I enjoyed her company and we talked of her research project on the study of eagles in this area. I shared many of my experiences with her, especially the spiritual ones. She asked about the concept of trail magic and if I had encountered any. Walking and talking with Christi had taken my mind off my aching feet, and I told her that trail magic could mean most any unexpected, pleasant event associated with one's walk on the trail. In fact, having met her would qualify as such an event.

After another 45-minute walk, I spotted something unusual on the side of the trail ... there, perched on a tree stump, set a cooler filled with sodas, grapes, bananas, and brownies. Now, Christi would experience the most complete offering of trail magic that I would encounter on the entire AT. The refreshments had been left on the trail by the parents of a former thru-hiker. This was their way to repay the kindness that others had shown their son. I signed the register that they had left, and it appeared that I was the third hiker to pass this way today.

We proceeded to a parking area where she had left her car and she offered me a ride into Hanover. As we crossed the Connecticut River, the state of Vermont was officially behind me. Christi drove me to the Dartmouth campus and let me out near Robinson Hall, where the Dartmouth Outing Club was located. I signed in and got oriented to the coed "fraternity" houses where I hoped to find lodging for a couple of nights. I was informed that one of the houses was off limits to hikers this particular weekend due to a party, and that the other houses were probably full. Things did not look good ... Hanover Inn, the only motel accommodation in town, charged $197. per night.

I made my way down the main street and turned right at a bank, heading to the Foley House. The house was unmarked and I walked past it the first time. When I walked up the steps on the wrap around front porch, I could see several packs, boots, and trekking poles and immediately knew that I must be in the right place. This house could only accommodate five hikers and there were already six who had signed in. The occupancy rule was not rigidly enforced, and one of the hikers planned to sleep on the front porch. I took a quick shower and made my way to the basement where the washer and dryer were located. I never encountered any of the students who resided at Foley; it was early afternoon and they must have been in class. *Paratrooper* was among the first five hikers to sign in; this would be our first get-together in almost a week. He was still on schedule doing 100 miles per week.

I decided to move on to the only other house left on my list, that being, Panarchy House. The house looked good from the outside, as two huge white pillars graced the front of the building. I made my way to the back of the building, where a homemade sign directed hikers to steps leading to a basement. Well, this was only the beginning of a weird and wacky two-night stay in "The Dungeon" ... their terminology, not ours! I seemed to be the first in and found myself a bed space near the door, so that I could see what I was doing. The basement had no electricity, so we were on our own with flashlights ... just like the trail.

We had the use of an upstairs bathroom with a shower, and could use the microwave and stove if we desired. My next priority was to get to the Post Office to pick up my food mail drop from home. As usual, Josephine had sent everything that I had requested, and then some; a former army buddy of mine had sent me two military rations (MRE). When I arrived back at "The Dungeon," several hikers had checked in ... *The Spice Girls* and three south-bounders from Canada, to include their trail dog, Lucky, were claiming their spaces for the night.

I went to dinner with the two women at an AYCE restaurant named, Every Thing But Anchovies. I really wasn't that hungry, as I had eaten off and on throughout the day. I returned to Panarchy House and sorted my food drop the best that I could, considering the lack of available light in "The Dungeon." Lucky's owner had gone to town and left him alone; he sat perched on one of the couches that served as a bed for anyone who would dare lay down in such filth. Lucky was without a doubt, the best-behaved trail dog that I would encounter on the entire AT; he posed for me as I took his picture.

By 2200, all hikers were in their sleeping bags in anticipation of a good nights sleep ... so much for that! Shortly after mid-night, all pandemonium broke loose on the hardwood floor above us. The rambunctious occupants of Panarchy House decided to party, and did they ever! The loud music blared and they roller bladed on the hardwood floor. Some were able to get some sleep, but I never did accomplish that much-desired state. The next morning, we all got a kick out of the commotion and decided that the occupants should change the name of their house to "Anarchy House." (mile 1,717.6)

DAY 146 – August 2, 1997
Today would be a busy one, as I ran all morning getting my packages ready to mail home. I was beginning to get rid of any equipment items that were not absolutely essential. I would be packing excess food out of Hanover, but I didn't care. I could always eat more than usual to lighten my load ... this would be a good problem to have. I ate breakfast at 0530 at a nearby convenience store and enjoyed talking with the attendant. I ate lunch at the Panda Restaurant and then went to a local grocery, where I purchased a few fill-in items for tomorrow's journey.

As I walked back to Panarchy House, I met *Paratrooper* heading out of town; he was continuing at a torrid pace in an effort to "put the trail behind him." This would mark the last time that I would see him until we would link up again in Gorham, NH. I ran into *Cycle Woman* on the way back; she was moving into Panarchy House, as the Foley House occupants planned a weekend party and asked the hikers to leave. *Partner* had rejoined her after arriving via AMTRACK ... his pack did not arrive with him, thus delaying their exit from Hanover until Monday.

I won't go into any detail, but Saturday night in "The Dungeon" was no different that Friday night ... in fact, the upstairs gang was even more energized than they were the night before. I tried to call home around 1930, but Josephine was not home. I plan to call her on my way out of Hanover tomorrow. I was dog-tired from lack of sleep, as well as my rigorous routines over the past two days. Not to complain ... my two-day experiences in this Ivy League college town would become one of my very favorite highlights of the trail. (mile 1,717.6)

Today was Saturday and I felt in a reflective mood, as I just lounged around Hanover and soaked up the atmosphere of this Ivy League college town. Although Vermont had been marked with long, arduous climbs, the state stood out vividly in my mind due to the diversity of its beauty. I walked through magnificent maple and pine forests, and occasionally, grassy clearings that we referred to as "balds," back in North Carolina and Virginia. The State of Virginia would now have to take a back seat; Vermont would become my favorite state among the fourteen that I would traverse on my 2,000-mile journey to Mt. Katahdin, Maine.

Hanover NH	
Glencliff NH	43.8 mi
Mt. Washington NH	109.2 mi
Gorham NH	143.3 mi
Andover ME	185.3 mi
Stratton ME	254.2 mi
Monson ME	327.9 mi
Mt. Katahdin ME	442.8 mi

-9-

UP WHERE WE BELONG
NEW HAMPSHIRE/MAINE

D AY 147 – August 3, 1997
I called home early this morning to talk with Josephine; she seemed resigned to my long absence and we were both counting the days until I returned. I had a great breakfast at Lou's Restaurant & Bakery and was headed out of Hanover at 0830. I glanced at my data book and was reminded of the sentiments of a 1987 north-bounder who stated, *"When you reach Hanover, you've done 80% of the miles, but you still have 50% of the work left."* With this encouraging thought in mind, I lowered my head and trudged on.

The first person that I met on the trail was a retired Army Colonel, who was out for his morning walk. He resided in Hanover and gave me a rundown on the history of this picturesque college town. Further up the trail, I met a south-bounder, by the name of *Mist-A-Shelter*. She had gotten her trail name from having missed so many shelters since beginning her journey at Mt. Katahdin, heading for Georgia. The weather looked threatening and a slight drizzle began to fall. I put a cover on my pack, primarily to fend against the moisture on the tree limbs that hung over the trail. I came off a steep descent and crossed a road to the next blaze leading past a small pond to my right. As I looked up, a bull moose was grazing in the shallows across the pond. He heard me before I could get my camera out of my pack and scampered off into the woods. I was disappointed and vowed to keep my camera more readily available through moose country.

I passed up Moose Mountain Shelter and walked another three miles before stopping at a creek for water. I moved on to Trapper John Shelter and pitched my tent for the evening. I had one of my military rations, beans and franks; not bad ... one thing about these "military delicacies," they are jam-packed with calories, but much heavier than the other main courses that I carry. I hope to leave camp by 0600 tomorrow. (mile 1,734.7)

DAY 148 – August 4, 1997
I departed camp at 0600 and immediately began climbing... just straight up! My intentions were to walk about 14 miles to Hexacuba Shelter, but when I finally reached the top of Smart's Mountain, I spotted the absolute best tent site that I had yet to encounter. It was only 1330 and the sun and blue skies,

105

combined with this great tent site, proved too much for me to pass up this idyllic spot. I pitched my tent on the only wooden platform in the area and marveled at the panoramic views that lay before me.

After I was fully situated, I walked a few hundred yards up the trail to the fire tower for a better view. The tower was in a poor state of repair, so I didn't push my luck by attempting to climb to the top. I found a good water source down a blue blazed trail leading to the Mike Murphy Spring. I returned to my tent site and at least two other thru-hikers had come in, only to be disappointed that I had occupied the only platform on Smart's Mountain. I picked up a weather report on my headset and the weather called for possible showers tonight, with sub-freezing temperature; I really didn't care, as I just wanted to soak up the sun and enjoy my very private setting.

I ventured down the trail to another unusual privy. This one was not fully enclosed and the occupant was clearly visible to all that might be passing by. The privy had a steering wheel and an old-fashioned window knob of the winding variety, located to the left and right of the toilet seat. Sometimes, one needs all of the humor possible to get through the hard times; this day would certainly not qualify as a "hard-time" day. I returned to my campsite and planned a 14-mile day for tomorrow. (mile 1,741.5)

DAY 149 – August 5, 1997

The weather report of yesterday held true … rained all night, but did not freeze. As I broke camp, I knew that this had been my best tenting experience, thus far. I was on the trail by 0630 and enjoyed lots of downhills with only a few climbs. When I arrived at Hexacuba Shelter, I met three section hikers from Georgia who planned to walk to Pinkham Notch, NH on this particular outing.

I filtered my water from a rushing stream in front of the shelter, as the three headed out ahead of me. We were all headed to Atwell Hill Road, where we planned to stay at the Atwell Hilton, a structure owned by the NPS, and closed several years ago. I caught up with the threesome and went ahead of them before we reached Atwell Road. Just before I reached the road, I spotted several bottles of clear, spring water setting by the side of the trail. They had been place there by Dizzy-B, a local trail angel, who catered to thru-hikers. I really didn't need water, but the thought of drinking bottled water after drinking from streams was too much to pass up. I dumped one liter of water and filled my bottle with the pure stuff.

I arrived at the Atwell Hilton a few minutes ahead of the Georgia hikers. It was drizzling rain and we sought shelter under a small overhang located at the end of the boarded up shelter. In a short while, Dizzy-B pulled up in her pick up truck and introduced herself. We had already figured out who she was. She asked if we were thirsty and proceeded to open the tailgate of her truck where she proudly displayed a cooler full of beer and sodas. *The Georgia Guys* went crazy ... they had not expected to refresh themselves with beer on this day. I consumed a couple of sodas, and we all dropped money in the jar that set next to the cooler.

We fired our stoves and proceeded to fix our evening meals; the rain had subsided and I pitched my tent in a weeded area that Dizzy-B had mowed, a few days earlier. There was not much level ground on which to pitch four tents, and we were all positioned side by side; it sort of reminded me of a military bivouac. I warned the trio that I was an early riser and would be up and out very early in the morning. We started a small bond fire with wood provided by Dizzy-B ... some kind of trail angel, huh? She hung around until it was nearly dark. One of the *Georgia Guys* asked her what the "B" stood for; she jokingly replied, "Anything you want it to be"... we laughed at the possibilities, and left it at that. I planned to get off at Glencliff tomorrow ... I hoped that my mail drop would be there. Josephine had never failed me, so I felt sure that I would not be disappointed tomorrow. (mile 1,752.8)

DAY 150 – August 6, 1997

I lived up to my reputation as an early riser ... I wasn't known as *Reveille* for nothing! At precisely 0445, I fired by stove and one of the *Georgia Guys* uttered and expletive that I wouldn't repeat. I had given them fair warning, thus I didn't feel too bad ... in fact, I sort of chuckled to myself, as I downed my customary morning oatmeal and coffee.

I left Atwell Road in search of the white blazed trail that would take me to the little village of Glencliff. It was only 0545, and I knocked out the 8.6 miles to Glencliff by 0930. The trail data book had been right on ... there were no services available, with the exception of the Post Office. It was located in a small white building that looked more like a garage than a U.S. Post Office. In fact, I walked right past the building before stopping at a house to ask a young boy for directions. Both of my packages were there; one from Josephine and the other that I had sent from Hanover.

A sign on the bulletin board indicated that sodas could be purchased at the front porch just up the road. I walked back up the road looking for a red roofed house and sure enough, there set the cooler; the sodas were only .75 cents and a note indicated that we were on the honor system. I tucked a dollar bill in the jar and walked back to the Post Office to sort my food.

I looked up and saw *Bird Man* coming up the road. After he secured his mail drop, we made plans to call the operator of a hostel who lived nearby to see if he had room for a one-night stay. Talk about luck ... Roger Brickner, an amateur meteorologist, dispatched a young man who was doing an internship with him for the summer. While we were awaiting our ride, Dizzy-B showed up to offer liquid refreshments and we eagerly partook.

After an hours wait, we were on our way to Roger's "House of Weather." This man turned out to be some kind of host. He showed us to the sleeping loft in the barn that was attached to his early 1800's estate house. He, then invited us into his home where we showered while he, the intern, and another friend of his, prepared horsd'oeuvres to be served on the patio of his aboveground swimming pool. *Bird Man* and I had thought that we had surely died and gone to heaven ... Roger even served wine with the finger food. We both passed up the invitation to swim and just reclined in the lounge chairs, hardly believing our good fortune.

Next, our gracious host prepared hamburgers served with salad and plenty of potato chips. He announced that he and his intern were leaving tomorrow for a flight to New York, where he had to make disposition on some property. Before we retired for the evening in our very own private barn loft, Roger informed us that we would have to be up early in the morning for the breakfast that he would personally prepare for us. *Bird Man* and I slept well as we attempted to absorb the events of the day. (mile 1,761.4)

DAY 151 – August 7, 1997
We departed Roger Brickner's home at 0730; the intern drove us back to the trailhead. Before he dropped us off, I asked him if Roger was a lawyer, and was surprised to learn that Roger had been a history teacher in a New York public school. This man was such a committed humanitarian; he had walked the entire AT a few years ago and had hosted over two thousand thru-hikers, as of 1997

Bird Man had to return to the Post Office, so I went ahead. I was back on the white blazed trail by 0815. Mt. Moosilauke, at 4,802-feet, would be my first climb on the AT that soared above treeline. My trail data book indicated that on a clear day, one could see five states from the summit. The day provided plenty of sunshine with a moderate breeze. I reached the summit alone, and the experience of being above tree line was exhilarating, to say the least. I removed my pack and leaned it against a signpost and took pictures, as the wind whipped against my flag. I needed a windbreaker when I stopped, but it was not long after resuming my walk that I stowed my jacket in my pack.

When I reached NH 112, Dizzy-B's cousin, a former thru-hiker, was there handing out Oreo cookies and sodas ... will this trail magic never end? ... I hope not! I departed for Kinsman Notch at 1427 ... straight up. I was about to enter the rugged White Mountain range. I met a southbound day hiker who informed me of a good campsite at Gordon Pond. He further indicated that I would probably see moose near the pond late in the evening or early in the morning. I walked the .3-mile side trail to Gordon Pond and set my tent up on level ground next to a fallen log.

Cycle Woman and *Partner* would come in about 30 minutes after I arrived and set up their tents right on the shoreline of the pond. They asked if I minded sharing my kitchen, a fallen log, and we prepared our evening meals together. This would be the beginning of a great friendship and we would hike together all the way to Gorham, NH. (mile 1,773.9)

DAY 151 – Mt. Moosilauke, 4,802 feet; my first above treeline climb.

DAY 152 – August 8, 1997

We left Gordon Pond at 0600 … never a moose did we see! Today brought some very vigorous climbs … hand-over hand, at times … straight up at times. I was beginning to believe the quote of the 1987 thru-hiker. I passed Eliza Brook Shelter and began the tough climb up South and North Kinsman Mountains. It was here that I met a lady and her son, Seddan and Reed Savage. We talked as we walked, and she offered me her bunk space at Lonesome Lake Hut; this was the first of several hut systems that span the AT through New Hampshire. She explained that they were leaving a day early and that the hut system would not refund her money. The accommodation included dinner and breakfast and normally cost $56. per day … talk about trail magic!

I went ahead, as she and her son were taking an alternate trail back to the hut. I waited for her at the kitchen where I was fortunate enough to get a huge portion of lasagna for $1. The hut system served leftovers on a first come, first served basis, and I was on a roll! Seddan and her son came in about an hour later, and informed the Hut Master of the arrangement. As it turned out, Seddan was a psychiatrist who specialized in addictions and pain relief ... she surely did wonders in relieving my pain! I thanked her and jotted her address on my data book, so that I could send her a thank you note. She recognized my gratitude and stated, "that I must be living right." WOW!

I was all set and moved into a two-person room with one of the summer employees. As I settled in, he strummed his guitar and entertained himself. My only concern now was to make North Woodstock by noon tomorrow in order to pick up my mail drop. To top of this incredible day, a couple and their grandson offered me a ride into North Woodstock tomorrow; I had to decline the offer, as I had to make the Post Office by noon, and they were not walking off the mountain until mid-morning. I was only 1.9 miles away from US 53, where I planned to hitch the 5.5 miles into North Woodstock. I would skip the hut breakfast in the morning in order to make it before the Post Office closed. (mile 1,784.2)

DAY 153 – August 9, 1997

I left Lonesome Lake Hut before 0530; it was only a short distance to the highway. There wasn't much traffic on US 53 and what few vehicles I saw passed me by. I began walking towards town and had proceeded about 1.5 miles, when a man and his wife in a pickup stopped. I hopped in the back of their truck and a few minutes later, they dropped me off in front of the Post Office.

After my customary off-trail pancake breakfast, I headed to the laundry and while my clothes were cycling, I walked across the street to the Post Office. Sure enough, my mail-ahead package that I had sent from Hanover was waiting for me. I returned to the laundry and sorted my food and mailed the excess to Monson, Maine. While waiting for my clothes to dry, I was approached by a young man in his early 30's, who had thru-hiked the AT in 1996. *Running Wind,* asked if I needed anything and I told him that I did need fuel. He left and came back with enough fuel to top me off, and gave me a bag of sweetened Kool-Aid. He had planned to give me a ride back to the trailhead, but got a phone page and had to alter his plans. I thanked him for his kindness and returned to the Post Office to mail my package.

I moved on to a convenience store where I bought a couple of sodas to take with me. As I was leaving the store, a young couple asked me how long I had been walking. They were impressed that I had walked slightly less than 1,800 miles since departing Georgia on March 10th. They had future plans to hike the AT and offered me a ride back to the trailhead. They let me out at the Flume Visitor Center, where Josephine and I had stopped last October. I called home and talked with her. She sounded so sad that I felt like packing it in and heading home.

As I made my way up the bike trail leading to the AT, I reflected on the events of the past two days, and how wonderful, caring people had gone out of their way to help me. Following my phone conversation with Josephine, I was beginning to feel a sense of sadness knowing that I was not home helping her as these total strangers had helped me.

The weather was nice and there were hordes of people on the trail for the weekend. I walked a very steep 2.7 miles to Liberty Springs Tent site, where I paid the $5. fee to pitch my tent on a wooden platform. *Cycle Woman* and *Partner* were already set up when I arrived. Tomorrow, we'll be above tree line, once again. (mile 1,789.5)

DAY 153 – Beginning a 2.7-mile climb to Liberty Springs Tentsite.

DAY 154 – August 10, 1997

I departed Liberty Springs Tentsite at 0615 and soon began the above tree-line trek. The weather was slightly hazy, but the breeze kept those pesky black flies at bay. I experienced some marvelous views from Mts. Lincoln, Lafayette, and Garfield. It was one mountain range after another, and the weather for the first half of the day could not have been better. I stopped at Galehead Hut where I had some lemonade and wrote a post card to Josephine.

The afternoon trek was arduous and I decided to put up at Mt. Guyot Campsite, located .6 mile off the AT. I got the next to last tent platform and paid the $5. fee. I seemed as tired as I had been since leaving Georgia. I was in terrific shape, but the climbs still took a toll on me this day. I planned a 10-mile walk for tomorrow … no need in attempting to push more than 7-10 miles per day through these rugged New Hampshire mountains. I shouldn't have difficulty sleeping tonight. (mile 1,802.8)

DAY 155 – August 11, 1997

Up early and on my way at 0631. I dreaded the .6 mile climb back to the AT junction; every additional mile seems to cause concern through this terrain. It took a little over 30 minutes to get back to the AT. I caught up with *Cycle Woman* and *Partner* by 0900; we walked to Zealand Falls Hut, where we had a coffee and the best walnut-pecan pie that I had ever eaten. By now you've probably noticed that I describe most non-trail food as, "the best I've ever eaten." The kitchen had no breakfast leftovers, but the pie did wonders to fill the void.

We departed in a light rain and headed for Ethan Pond Campsite. We tented after rendering the usual fee; many thru-hikers had developed a negative attitude towards the Appalachian Maintenance Club (AMC). This section through New Hampshire was the only place on the entire AT where one was required to pay for pitching a tent. Many times, the tent platforms were already occupied and the caretakers would permit camping in overflow area. For the most part, these overflow areas were entirely unsuitable and sometimes unsanitary, yet required the same $5. fee. To put it bluntly, the AMC Hut system was designed for people of means who could afford the fees at the lodges that spanned the Presidential and White Mountain Ranges. I suppose that I'm overreacting to the AMC, and perhaps, I'm really out of sorts due to this rugged, challenging terrain. Tomorrow's trek would take us back to civilization, and we looked forward to getting off the trail at Crawford Notch, US 302. (mile 1,811.4)

DAY 156 – August 12, 1997

I was on the trail at 0745 and enjoyed the 2.9-mile downhill trek to US 302.

I set out to walk the one-mile distance to the Wiley House. They did not open until 0900, so I spread my wet tent on a picnic table in hopes that it would dry. You'd be surprise how much weight the wet gear adds to pack weight. In a short while, *Partner* and *Cycle Woman* pulled up ... they had gotten a lift from a man who stopped to offer them a ride. This couple had a real knack for acquiring rides without so much as sticking out their thumbs. I kidded them and attributed their good fortune being related to their "senior citizen" status; neither revealed their age, but I suspected that I was a couple of years older than they. We enjoyed a good breakfast and I must have consumed 3-4 cups of coffee ... bought several Snickers and carried out a sandwich for the big climb. I called home and talked with Josephine; she seemed amazed that I had now walked all the way to where we had stopped last October.

We were about to enter the 25-mile Presidential Range that ran all the way to Pinkham Notch. A young lady befriended us at the snack bar and related that she had thru-hiked the AT several years ago. She shuttled the three of us back to the trailhead, where we reluctantly hit the trail to enter the Presidentials. I met *Sandal Man* on the first climb ... he walked in sandals in lieu of boots. I could hardly believe that his feet and ankles would bear up under the rigors of the trail. He indicated that he was on his third pair and that his footwear, to this point, had cost him less than $50. He moved ahead of us and was soon out of sight.

I thought that I would never reach the summit of the first climb. The view back to Crawford Notch and US 302 was awe-inspiring. We passed over Mts. Webster and Jackson heading for Mizpah Spring Hut, where we pitched our tents at Nauman Tentsite. All of the platforms had been taken and the caretaker walked us to an overflow area ... this was literally, the absolute pits! The area had once been used as a privy site and still carried waste from the hut area ... the stench was so bad that we almost declined to tent here. The alternative would be to move on to the next authorized tenting area, and none of us wanted to face another climb on this day. We begrudgingly paid our fees and settled in for the night. Tomorrow's itinerary called for us to climb Mts. Pierce and Washington, with a stop at Lakes of the Cloud Hut for food and drink. We hoped to get over Mt. Washington before the rains hit. (mile 1,820.6)

DAY 157 – August 13, 1997

We left Nauman Tentsite at 0600 heading for Mt. Washington. Around 0747, the weather turned foul with gusting wind and driving rain. I had begun the day in shorts and tee shirt, and soon made my first change to a windbreaker. After a short distance, I became concerned about hypothermia, and stopped to put on full rain gear over my polar tech outing gear. I had to take cover behind a huge boulder, as the rain and wind was absolutely fierce. As I continue climbing, I was almost blown off my feet on several occasions.

I arrived at Lakes of the Cloud Hut around 0945. I was chilled to the bone and even though the hut had no heating system, it sure beat being out in the elements on this day. *Young-man* and *Sleepy* had stayed the night at the hut and were preparing to move on to the summit of Mt. Washington. They had done a work-for-stay at the hut, and *Cycle Woman, Partner, Running Wild, Four Winds,* and I decided to do the same; we were lucky to get the last five available slots.

As we sat in the lounge area awaiting our work assignments, some tourist hikers with small children came in seeking shelter from the elements. *The Spice Girls* came in around 1130 and reported that they had passed a grown man who was in tears. It was mind boggling to think that anyone would venture through the White Mountains without proper gear. Every trailhead had signs warning hikers of the danger associated with unexpected severe weather. Even at that, some treated the AT as just another "stroll in the park."

A couple of fellow thru-hikers decided to take an alternate blue blazed trail leading to Pinkham Notch, thus avoiding Mt. Washington. The hut staff warned that this trail could be treacherous in bad weather, but the two headed out anyway. I was so thankful for a bunk, food, and most of all, protection from the elements. Hopefully, tomorrow will bring better weather. The hut was very damp and cold, and we wrapped ourselves in blankets in an effort to stay warm. The hut was packed out for the night and there was lots of commotion, as people scurried about the main lobby.

My chores were scheduled for tomorrow morning; I was to set the tables and assist the kitchen help with whatever needed to be accomplished. There was plenty of food available and the brownies sure went down good ... all that I needed was a quart of milk. I turned in early in an effort to get warm ... never did, as my sleeping bag and clothes were damp from the day's rain. I located some extra blankets and gave them *to The Spice Girls,* who planned to sleep on the floor. They both got a charge out of me, a retired Lieutenant Colonel, pulling KP. I planned to do 10.1 miles tomorrow to Osgood Tentsite beyond Mt. Washington Observatory. I was really optimistic and looking to be in Gorham, NH in three days. (mile 1,825.3)

DAY 158 – August 14, 1997

We finished with our chores and had a big breakfast ... we felt fortunate to have been able to do a work-for-stay. We departed Lakes of the Cloud Hut at 0940 on our way up Mt. Washington. Today was a carbon copy of yesterday ... heavy fog, and biting wind. It took one hour to walk the 1.4 miles to the summit of Mt. Washington. The wind blew my bandana off the loop of my shoulder strap and I didn't even know it.

On April 12, 1934, the weather station atop Mt. Washington clocked the highest surface wind ever recorded, at 231 mph. When we reached the summit, everything was socked in with visibility at zero! *Cycle Woman, Partner* and I made our way to the visitors complex next to the weather observatory and located the food bar. *Partner* had mailed a food drop to the small Post Office at the visitor's center; the Postal Clerk was extremely rude to thru-hikers, as he begrudgingly sorted through mounds of packages in search of a particular name.

As we sat eating our mid-morning lunch, *Cycle Woman* suggested that we take an alternate blue blazed trail off Mt. Washington, as the weather forecast for the day looked horrible. We decided to go for it, as several other hikers took shuttle vans to Pinkham Notch Visitors Center to escape the foul weather. No one wanted to risk hypothermia by continuing on to Osgood Tentsite, some 14 miles ahead.

The trail that we opted for was designated as a wilderness trail, and we would not have attempted it without the topographic maps that *Partner* was carrying. We purchased extra sandwiches and headed for the blue blazed trail, just beyond the observatory. We made our way across the Cog Railroad tracks, and headed straight down into this deep canyon. As we made our descent, I took the lead and we slowly wound our way over huge boulders and loose rocks. On several occasions, I wondered what we had gotten ourselves into. We knew that the wilderness trail would eventually join the AT near the West Branch, Peabody River. *Cycle Woman* was having a great deal of difficulty; *Partner* left his pack about halfway down to return to carry her pack for her. She wore a heavy brace on her left leg due to an old sports injury, but she was totally committed to hiking the entire AT in one season. In fact, she had ridden a bicycle from coast to coast a few years back, and that is how she came to be known as *Cycle Woman*. One good thing about this trail ... there were no tourists down here.

It took me two hours to reached the canyon floor. I spotted the two as they slowly wound their way downward, and I climbed back up a short ways to assist *Cycle Woman* with her pack. The trail continued along a rain-swollen stream and at times, we were walking in water over our boots. This would definitely have been a bad experience if we had not had the detailed topographic map of the area. We walked until 1630 and found a fairly good area to pitch our tents. At day's end, we could hardly believe what we had done. Looking back towards Mt. Washington, we could barely make out any of the buildings. We planned an early start tomorrow and looked forward to seeing white blazes, again. (mile 1,832.3)

DAY 159 – August 15, 1997

We left camp at 0615. *Partner* seemed to be struggling and related that he felt weak. He was probably still suffering some ill effects from the Lyme disease that had compelled him to come off the trail back in PA. We wound our way along what we took to be the Peabody River, hoping that it would bring us out on the AT. Atlas ... we picked up the white blazed trail and proceeded across a footbridge; we had gone only a few hundred yards when *Partner* exclaimed, "I think we are heading southward towards Mt. Washington." We stopped dead in our tracks and reviewed the map, again. Sure enough, we were headed in the opposite direction of Pinkham Notch. No harm done ... thanks to *Partner's* orienteering skills. My thoughts raced back to that dreadful day of June 18th when I got turned around on the AT and walked an additional 4-5 miles before I made it to Duncannon, PA.

We lightened up quite a bit after we knew that we were finally out of the wilderness; we arrived at Pinkham Notch Visitors Center at 1100. *The Spice Girls*, *Young-man*, *Sleepy*, and *Bird Man* were already at the center. I learned that *Paratrooper* was only a day or so ahead, and was walking with *Sun Brite*. We had an AYCE lunch for $6. and really pigged out. The three of us back-tracked on the AT for .2 miles where we pitched our tents so far back in the woods that no one could possible spot us. This wooded area was the only area that we were permitted to camp and the AMC tenting regulations were rigidly enforced. I turned in early this evening and sort of dreaded Wildcat Mountain, the next major climb. (mile 1,840.1)

Day 160 – August 16, 1997

I had the AYCE breakfast at the Center while *Cycle Woman* and *Partner* decided to bypass the meal and left before I was ready to depart. I was back on the trail by 0815. The climb up Wildcat Mountain was as difficult as had been projected. On the way up I came upon six young women from a neighboring town; some of them were seasoned hikers, while a few had never been on a trail in their lives. One of the hikers was lagging behind and the others were attempting to give her encouragement. She was directly ahead of me and was apparently suffering from acrophobia; she was afraid to look down and was sort of frozen in place. The friends told her to close her eyes and grab the rock in front of her in order to pull herself forward. The frightened young lady replied, "God, I'd rather have another baby than do this!" I was right behind her and jokingly said, "Don't you dare have that baby here." They all laughed and she moved ahead; she couldn't get over the way I was standing up and walking the rock cliffs that she had been hugging while on her knees. I explained to her that I had a little over 1,800 miles of practice, so she should not feel bad.

I could only average about a mile an hour through this mountainous stretch. I passed *Cycle Woman* and *Partner* on my way to Carter Notch Hut, where I stopped a 1330 to replenish my water. I talked with some weekenders and moved on towards Zeta Pass. I arrived there around 1630 and searched the area for a tent site. A father and his two young sons had already made camp and I set up about 100 yards from them. I went back to the trail and left a note for *Cycle Woman* and *Partner* ... they came in about 45 minutes later and made their way to my camp. We fixed our evening meals and crashed. (mile 1,853.2)

DAY 161 – August 17, 1997

I was up and out by 0715 and on my way to Gorham; I was halfway considering pitching my tent at Rattle River Shelter. I had heard several good comments regarding the swimming holes on the river and the abundance of good campsites. It would only be a 10.6-mile walk to the shelter and I could be there around noon. The downhills were steep and very slippery from the recent rains. I took another hard spill this morning ... no harm done!

Shortly after my fall, I spotted *Paratrooper* on the trail ahead of me. He was walking very deliberately, and I immediately knew that he had received another injury. He stopped in his tracks when I greeted him; we were both excited to see each other. As we walked, I talked of my indecisiveness regarding tenting on the river vs. going ahead to Gorham. We walked together for a while and the trail seemed to level out. I went ahead to the shelter to scout out the river. In a short while, *Paratrooper* came in and he seemed to have perked up when he hit the level portion of the trail. He recounted how he had fallen and jammed his shoulder; his knees were also bothering him. We sat down at the shelter to talk about our evening destination. The next 1.9 miles to US 2 was good trail, so we decided to go for Gorham. A jogger that we had met on the trail was about to leave the parking area, and he agreed to give us a lift into Gorham.

We checked into the Libby House Bed & Breakfast before noon. The majority of our fellow hikers were headed to Hiker's Paradise, a favorite stopover for the trail-hip. This was the last type of hostel that the two of us needed, as the B&B seemed perfectly suited to us. The Libby House was built at the turn of the century, when the logging industry was at its peak. This was the most elaborate B&B that I stayed in while on the trail. We shared a two-bedroom suite on the third floor; Maggie, the hostess, was a very kind lady who had a young baby. We had a private bath with the largest, fluffiest towels that I had seen in a long while.

It was off to town for some additional supplies; I ran into *The Spice Girls*, *Sir Lancelot, Cycle Woman* and *Partner*. They were all riding bicycles that had been provided for them at Hiker's Paradise, where they were staying. We both turned in early after a full day's agenda. The best was yet to come … another day off the trail with some last minute preparations for the trek into Maine. (mile 1,860.9)

DAY 162 – August 18, 1997

I was up early, 0500, to be exact, and went to a nearby convenience store for coffee; this was the same convenience store where I had purchased coffee the day before. I laid my $1.03 on the counter for the coffee and the attendant stated, "Just take it." I was taken back by his offer and again attempted to pay for the coffee; once again, he declined my offer, and I left with the coffee. *Paratrooper* and I got a real laugh out of my encounter … after all, I thought that I looked fairly presentable, and now I realized that I must have qualified as a certified "trail bum."

I sat on a bench at the City Park and watched the town wake up. I really enjoyed this quiet little New Hampshire hamlet. We had to wait until 0730 for Maggie to serve all of the guests at once; she fixed Belgium waffles, bacon, muffins, melon, juice and coffee. Around mid-morning, Maggie's husband gave us a ride to the local grocery that was about five miles away. We sorted our rations and made plans for our final push into Maine and the long awaited "hundred-mile wilderness," that would lead us to Mt. Katahdin.

As we brainstormed our itinerary, it suddenly became apparent that planning food drops was becoming more difficult. Josephine would send me the final mail drop from home to arrive at Monson, ME. It was up to me to take care of the next two drops at Andover and Stratton, ME. We knew that it would be better to have too much food at these drops as we could always send the extra food ahead, or give it away. It took me all morning to shop, package and mail the three boxes of supplies. In the afternoon, I shopped for fuel, insect repellent, and last minute snacks.

Around 1500, I toured the Gorham Railroad Museum that still operates a freight train through the town. A major hotel used to set on land now utilized as a city park. Speaking of the park, I found a swing and just sat there soaking up the afternoon sun. The warm breeze felt so food after enduring the cold winds and rain of a few days ago in the White Mountains. A freight train passed in front of me and I counted 40 cars in all; I could get used to this little town.

I ran into *Sir Lancelot* who had developed knee problems in the Whites. He had purchased fiberglass trekking poles in an effort to curb the stress being placed on his knees. I asked him to suggest this remedy to *Paratrooper* ... he did, and as expected, he decided to have nothing to do with using any type of "crutch" on his way to Katahdin. I had to look in a mirror to see another person like *"Paratrooper."*

That evening, we ate at an Italian Restaurant that Maggie's husband had recommended. The food was rather bland for Italian cuisine, and I wished that I had opted for burger and fries. We tolerated a lot of shortcomings on the trail, but sorry restaurant food just wouldn't hack it. These two days off in Gorham were truly a blessing; the day had been full of activities, and I honestly did not feel rested ... nonetheless, I felt content at day's end. (mile 1,860.9)

DAY 163 - August 19, 1997

Following another great breakfast-by-Maggie, the painter who worked for his keep at the B&B, drove us back to the trailhead. Maggie's husband and his dog had spent the night back at Rattle River Shelter and the painter planned to pick him up at the point where he would drop us off. We thanked him for the ride and set out on the AT, around 0820.

I walked ahead of *Paratrooper,* and soon met up with *Cycle Woman* and *Sun Brite*; they were slacking towards Gorham. *Cycle Woman* informed me that *Partner* had left the trail at Gorham and returned to his home in DC. He never fully recovered from the Lyme disease that he contracted back in PA. I would surely miss him as he was a dedicated hiker ... no slacking for this man! Today was a beautiful sunny day with mild temperatures ... hardly sweated, even on the climbs. I met *Rip,* a Knoxville, TN resident, who was thru-hiking the AT. His girlfriend was providing transportation for him and two pals, as they planned to slack most of the remaining miles to Mt. Katahdin. We talked Big Orange football for a while and I moved on with *Bo-Bo;* she was a strong hiker who had been traveling with *Rip* and the others. We pushed ahead, eagerly watching for the sign that would mark our entrance into the great state of Maine. I pitched my tent at Gentian Pond Campsite. *Paratrooper*, *Sir Lancelot*, *Young-man*, *Sleepy*, *The Spice Girls* and *Bo-Bo* camped here, also. As I turned in for the night, I thought ahead and wondered if the Mahoosic Notch was really as treacherous as most southbound hikers had reported. (mile 1,872.9)

DAY 164 – August 20, 1997

I departed camp at 0615 heading for Full Goose Shelter, a hard 10 miles of short, steep climbs. The descents were very slippery and the rock faces were hard to negotiate. Today, we would cross over into Maine and that made the day a memorable one. *Bo-Bo* and I had crossed the state line together and we proudly posed for pictures that would verify that we had now entered our 14th, and last state, since departing Georgia way back in March.

We did lots of marshy walking on the 4x6x8 planks that were so slippery that one could take a spill even though exercising all possible caution. I arrived ahead of the others, and got my choice of tent platforms. *Bo-Bo* came in next, followed by *Young-man* and a troupe of Boy Scouts, who occupied the entire shelter … there would be lots of disappointed thru-hikers tonight. *Paratrooper* was the last to come in, and he seemed so fatigued that I got his water for him. He indicated that he was considering staying at the shelter for another day before tackling the Mahoosic Notch. I thought that this was a good decision, as a group of southbound day hikers had reported that rain was forecast for the next two days. What else is new? I settled in early with plans to depart camp by 0530. One thing for sure, I wanted to get through the Notch before the rains hit! (mile 1,882.7)

DAY 165 – August 21, 1997

True to plans, I was ready to depart Full Goose Shelter at 0530. I had to use my flashlight to spot the trail. I knew that the rains would surely come, as I hurried toward the Mahoosic Notch. My plans called for me to set down at Speck Pond Campsite … only 5.1 miles ahead.

Before I realized it, I was staring directly at this gigantic mound of rocks that resembled a canyon. I knew in a heartbeat that one miscalculated step on these boxcar-sized boulders could mean the end of my journey. I prayed silently for the Holy Spirit's guidance, as I took my first cautious step into the Notch. It would have been nice to have a partner when traversing this treacherous stretch of terrain.

The trail data book had warned hikers to stay on the high side of the rocks, as much as possible. There were times when I had to stop dead in my tracks and just think about the consequences of what might happen if I missed a step. It began to sprinkle rain after I had zigzagged my way for about 45 minutes. I was thankful that I had been able to enter the canyon without the additional hazard of rain slickened rocks. On occasions, I could not stay on the high side and had to resort to lowering myself to the streambed that flowed under these giant rocks. It finally happened … about mid-way through this 1.1-mile obstacle course, I fell and landed on my left side. I broke the brunt of my fall with my left hand and arm; my trusty pack, once again, absorbed a major portion of the impact. It happened so quickly that I seemed a little stunned; I surveyed my left side to see what damage had been done. I was relieved that I could move my left wrist and fingers, however, my hand was already puffy and my left palm was turning blue.

I was thankful for not being more seriously injured and wished above all else that *Paratrooper* would not attempt to maneuver the Notch on this day.

I moved on with even more caution, if that was possible. I thought that I would never reach the east end of the Notch, and just as I did, it commenced to rain hard, and the wind picked up. Two southbound hikers passed me just before I began the steep climb up the Mahoosic Arm that would lead me to Speck Pond Shelter and Campsite. The wind and rain would normally have caused me to lament the bad weather; just getting through the Notch in one piece was so rewarding that I was thankful for anything that the trail had to offer.

The Arm was just as steep as expected, and the fog was beginning to settle in all around me. At this juncture, I seemed to have lost my sense of time and focused on my footing, as I climbed over rocks and roots on my way to the shelter. When I finally reached the shelter, I glanced at my watch in disbelief. I had traveled 5.1 miles through some of the most hazardous terrain on the AT, in 4 hrs. and 40 minutes. I was entirely drenched and the wind was picking up considerably. Once again, the thought of hypothermia ran through my mind, as I got out of my wet clothes and into my sleeping bag. I moved to the driest corner of the shelter and boiled some water for coffee. The rain slacked a bit, and I decided to find the site caretaker, and pay my fee. This would be my very last time to pay for shelter or tent site accommodations.

The caretaker was a young college student who offered me some food that had been left behind by a section hiker; this included bread, chicken salad, and some grapes. I gladly took the food and made my way back to the shelter, where I decided to go ahead and pitch my tent in lieu of staying in the shelter. I had no more than anchored my tent on one of the wooden platforms, when the wind began gusting so hard that I feared that my tent would be blown away; the rains came in squalls. I could hear voices at the shelter and they would turn out to be *Sir Lancelot*, *The Spice Girls*, *Young-man*, *Sleepy*, and *Bo-Bo*.

The caretaker told them of the food that she had given to me and it wasn't long before I could hear chants to the effect that, "*Reveille* has probably eaten all of the food!" I had eaten a single sandwich and some of the grapes. *Sir Lancelot* had set up on a platform next to me and between squalls, I passed the food on to him … he shared the remainder of the food with our wet, hungry companions who were huddled in the shelter. As I lay in my relatively dry tent, I was thankful that we had all made it though this trying day … perhaps the worst day since Georgia. I managed to stay warm and ate most of my food, except for the rations that I would need to get me to Andover, ME.

At the close of this challenging day, I realized that I was camped at Speck Pond. This beautiful alpine pond was billed as the highest in the State of Maine.

I was disappointed to think that I never got a glance at this body of water due to the driving rain and fog. Oh well, tomorrow will surely be a better day. (mile 1,887.8)

DAY'S 166/167 – August 22-23, 1997
    I left speck Pond at 0445 and walked in a driving rain most of the morning. The trail was full of water and it was just like walking in a creek bed ... boots completely submerged at times. To add to the misery, the steep downhills were extremely slippery. I held on to trees and roots as I slowly inched my way northward toward Katahdin. Sometimes, it was only the thought of standing on that final mountaintop that kept me going.
    Surprisingly, I traversed the steepest portions of today's trail without falling a single time. My left palm was now a deep purple and stiff from yesterday's fall in the Notch. I arrived at Bald Pate Lean-to around 1100. I attempted to dry my water soaked tent to no avail, so I moved on to Frye Notch Lean-to, where I filtered some water. I decided to go for Andover, as I was totally drenched and out of sorts from the travails of the past two days. The trail was very difficult, as I plodded and plunged by way through bogs and streams.
    Just when I was beginning to wonder if I would ever reach a solid roadbed again, I set foot on Andover East B Road. As one would expect in the backwoods of Maine, a portion of this road leading into Andover was merely a dirt road. The harsh winters and logging trucks certainly take a toll on the State's highway system. It was 1730 when I started hitching a ride into Andover. Several pickup trucks passed without the offer of a ride. After about 45 minutes, I decided to set out on the 8-mile trek into Andover. My contingency plan was to camp in the woods off to the side of the road, if I couldn't make the 8 miles by dark. There was a rain-swollen creek to the left of the road, so I wouldn't have to worry about water for my evening meal.
    After walking for a mile or two, I spotted a mini-van approaching me from the direction of Andover. Since the van was heading in the opposite direction, I didn't pay much attention until the driver slowed and turned around in front of me. I was greeted by the friendly voices of Earl and Margie Towne of Andover. As Earl assisted me with loading my pack in the van, he stated, "The Lord told us to come." I was not terribly surprised, as I had told myself all day that He would provide. I told the Towne's that I was headed for the Andover Arms Bed & Breakfast and they asked me if I had reservations. I did not, and thought that this might mean trouble should the B&B not have a room available. After learning that I had no arrangement, the Towne's invited me to stay in the basement apartment of their log home. I was a little uneasy in taking them up on this offer,

122

but I agreed, and Earl stopped at the Post Office, so that I could pick up my mail drop.

As we headed toward the Towne's place, Margie invited me to eat the evening meal with them ... Alaska salmon with salad, veggies, and desert. For someone who was soaked head to toe and had walked 16.9 miles today, this offer was too good to be true. Earl showed me to the first floor of their log home and I settled in and hung my wet rain gear near the wood stove. Earl then led me to a storage area where he and Margie kept assorted clothing for hikers who had not a dry garment. The Towne's also provided a washer and dryer for us, as well as a kitchen area ... oh yes, a shower and commode, the most important accessory of all. What a blessing! The accommodations also included a TV, couch, and a dinning table; the Towne's had lived in this level for about two years while Earl finished the two floors directly above. As we finished the strawberry ice cream that Margie served for desert, Earl was already planning coffee for early morning. I could hardly believe their hospitality ... what great Christian people!

I excused myself early and stoked the wood stove in an effort to generate enough heat to dry my wet gear. I washed my dirty clothes and wondered if *Paratrooper* had attempted to make it through the Notch. He was the only thru-hiker that I knew that had planned to pick up a mail drop in Andover, so I knew that he would be coming in. Earl had asked me about others who might be headed into Andover, and I told him of my concern for *Paratrooper*. I made preliminary plans to leave the next day and I informed the Towne's that I wanted to take them to breakfast at the local town restaurant. They accepted my offer and it was off to bed for me. Lightening, thunder, and heavy rain pelted all about, and I tossed and turned most of the night. One thing for sure, I had been truly blessed by the kindness of Earl and Margie Towne, and I knew from whence it came.

I was up early and I could hear Earl stirring above as he readied the coffee; this would turn out to be a day marked by a series of stunning events. At day's end, the others, and I would surely know that these events were not left to chance. Earl, Margie, and I left for the only restaurant in town and settled in for a heaping breakfast of pancakes with all the trimmings. Just as we were about to get down to some serious eating, in walked *The Spice Girls,* and we invited them to take breakfast with us. The Towne's never met a stranger, and began asking about their plans, and if any other hikers were with them. As it turned out, the girls, *Young-man, Sleepy,* and *Bo-Bo* were planning to stay at the Andover B&B. True to form, the Towne's offered the use of their apartment and *The Spice Girls* left after breakfast to inform the others of the offer.

As the Towne's and I returned to their place, we discussed the plight of

Paratrooper and how we might find him on the trail. Earl and Margie had been planning a hike when they had found me yesterday. They decided to go to the obvious trail location where *Paratrooper* might possibly be, if he was able to make it to Andover B Hill Road. This would kill two birds with one stone ... drop off the others who planned to slack and look for our friend, *Paratrooper*, at the same time. The Towne's drove their van and Earl asked me to haul the five hikers in his older panel van that he use for just this purpose. It was off to the trailhead where we dropped the slackers off and Earl and Margie made ready to walk southbound on the AT in search of *Paratrooper*. While we were planning our pickup strategy for the others, two north bounders approached us. We asked if they had seen a hiker by the name of *Paratrooper*. They indicated that he was about 2-3 miles back on the trail, and that he had fallen in the Notch and injured himself pretty badly. They assured us that he was on his feet and headed in our direction. Earl and Margie decided to go and bring him out and that I would back track to see if Sir Lancelot had made it off the trail.

I returned to Andover to shop for groceries, so that I could make a corn chowder and a bowl of trifle for our evening meal; everyone would be famished at day's end and I was the designated cook. All was looking good ... we would have *Paratrooper* off the trail soon and the others were doing their thing. Now, all that we needed was to round up *Sir Lancelot,* and this could be the making of a perfect day.

I headed towards Andover and as I approached the AT where it intersected the highway, I spotted *Sir Lancelot,* standing on the road with his thumb extended. I will never forget the look on his face when I stopped to offer him a ride. His smile smacked of disbelief as I opened the rear doors of the van, so that he could stow his pack. It took him a minute or so to respond and we gave each other high five's, as I cranked the van and headed for Andover. I related my experiences of the past two days and shared my faith that God had surely ordained this conclave of hikers who would gather this evening at the Towne's. Once again, it was obvious to me that the Holy Spirit was at work, and none of this had taken place through chance or luck.

Sir Lancelot was starved and we went to the restaurant where he ate a double order of pancakes. He later admitted that the quantity of food almost made him sick. We left for the Towne's home where he laid out his wet gear and I showed him to our accommodations ... was he ever impressed! While he showered, I aired out some of *The Spice Girl's* equipment, as the sun had begun to break through. We returned to town to shop for food. Tomorrow would be *Ginger's* 40th birthday, and *Sir Lancelot* wanted to surprise her with a birthday cake. We returned to the homestead and I hurried about fixing the chowder and desert. *Sir Lancelot* agreed to drive the van back to the trailhead to pick up the rest of the gang, while I finished preparing the evening meal.

In about an hour, he returned with the others and soon after, the Towne's pulled up with *Paratrooper*. As we went to the van to greet him, he related that he had fallen and bruised his chest and back. The Towne's asked me to take their van and transport him to a hospital in Rumford, the nearest town, about 25 miles southeast of Andover. Much to our relief, he had no broken bones, but had suffered some internal bruising. The doctor advised him to rest for 5-6 days, but I knew that this would not set well with this "ole marine." He reluctantly promised me that he would not return to the trail until he could manage a pack. I suggested that he try slack packing until he could recover sufficiently to accommodate a full pack.

When we arrived back at the Towne's, everyone came out to greet us, and they rejoiced knowing the *Paratrooper* had not suffered a trail ending injury. We topped off this eventful day with the food that I had prepared, plus some extras that Margie and Earl threw in. We sang happy birthday to *Ginger*, and we all crashed early that evening. So much had transpired since I had left Speck Pond two days ago that it made my head swim to think about it. Not to worry ... the Holy Spirit had everything under control and all that was left was to give praise for all of the bestowed blessings. Tomorrow, we would all move ahead with the exception of *Paratrooper,* who would convalesce with the Towne's. (mile 1,902.9)

DAY 167 – Earl and Margie Towne of Andover, Maine. This wonderful couple hosted eight very weary hikers for two days. Their kindness and generosity was the highlight of my journey. They have since opened a hostel, **The Cabin**, and minister to hikers on a year-round basis.

DAY 168 – August 24, 1997

Paratrooper invited everyone to breakfast this morning; this was a time of mixed emotions. The Towne's had been such marvelous hosts, and we were all reconstituted by their hospitality. If only my close friend was able to travel with us. Still, we had so much to be thankful for, especially the fact that he had suffered no permanent injuries. I hoped that he would listen to his body and not his Marine Corps mind. We were all ready for transportation back to the trailhead. I would be at least a half-day behind the others since they had slacked ahead on the trail yesterday. *Paratrooper* drove us all to our destinations; he seemed somewhat dejected when we all departed. I wasn't sure that I had said enough as we departed, but I tried to offer him encouragement without giving him the idea that he was all right, and could continue at the same pace as the rest of us. This would be the last time that I would walk with him, but he would remain in my thoughts and prayers as I plodded my way to Mt. Katahdin.

I arrived at South Arm Road around 1600 and tented near a stream. *Spam* and *Smoke'n* came in shortly after my arrival and set up beside me. I discovered that I had forgotten to top off my fuel in Andover. In the busy hub-bub of the past two days, I had taken better care of the others than I had myself ... oh well, I had no doubt the Lord would provide, as always. I had only walked 10.2 miles today due to the late start. Old Blue Mountain lay directly ahead and it was judged to be a bear of a climb ... one that I would not tackle on this day! (mile 1,913.1)

DAY 169 – August 25, 1997
I left camp at 0608 and headed up Old Blue Mountain ... straight up for three miles. Next, I climbed Bemis Mountain and stopped at the shelter for water. Water was never a problem through Maine, as the streams and rivers were full from the run off of several weeks of rain. As I moved forward, I wondered how I would fair in fording the rain-swollen streams ahead. According to my data book, there would be several streams to cross without the luxury of footbridges.

I arrived at Sabbath Day Pond Lean-to around 1730 ... wet and dog tired. I had gotten wind that several "thru-hikers" had bypassed this difficult section of the AT ... not that I wasn't tempted. It was here that I encountered the first African American hiker on the AT. He had flip-flopped and was now headed south to where he had left the trail to travel to Mt. Katahdin. His trail name was *Sarge*, and he had spent 11 years in the Marine Corps ... he sure was a talker and kept the shelter occupants in stitches with trail spun yarns. I pitched my tent in a pouring rain and settled in for the night. (mile 1,930.0)

DAY 170 – August 26, 1997
I awakened to a beautiful day and left camp at 0630. The trail bordered South Pond and I kept my eyes peeled for signs of moose, as this was definitely moose country. As I pushed ahead, I knew that *Spam*, *Smoke'n*, *Young-man*, and *Sleepy* were right behind me. My usual early starts gave me a little edge on these young whippersnappers, before they would eventually blow by me. We were now traveling, as a group, and all but *Smoke'n* would stand atop Mt. Katahdin with me after our final climb.

I stopped at a pond for a snack and set my pack down to go to the waters edge to filter some water. I heard a chattering commotion near my pack and hurried back to see what was happening. A red squirrel had decided that I had invaded its territory and was running about the ground and trees to let me know of my intrusion. I threw it a cracker and he quickly gathered it in and set off for his den, where he stored it and returned for more. He was so cute that I could not resist throwing him more crackers. I had to tell myself that I had better stop, as I was running low on snacks, myself. I took his picture and moved on.

The trail had leveled somewhat around the pond areas, but there would be several short climbs before I would reach Eddy Pond. At times, the trail seemed more like a bike trail than a rugged backcountry pathway. I supposed that I had walked for so long on challenging terrain, that anything less than hand-over-hand climbing and dangerous descents, seemed like a piece of cake. When I arrived at Maine 4, *Spam*, *Smoke'n*, and *Young-man* were attempting to hitch to Rangeley for resupply. I purchased *Spam's* fuel, as he could resupply when he reached Rangeley.

I went ahead to Piazza Rock Lean-to. I filtered some water and moved on to Eddy Pond, where I would tent on a fabulous pond known for its moose inhabitants. It was only 1500 when I set down and made my way to a large rock aside the pond. There were several large rocks sticking out of the shallow water, and one of the rocks seemed to move. It was a huge bull moose frolicking in the water on the far side of the pond. He was almost completely submerged as he dredged the bottom for plankton. He would occasionally toss his head, as if to rid himself of the pesky mosquitoes that were everywhere. I sat there in the sun and just enjoyed this unusual site of spotting a feeding moose in the mid-afternoon.

I washed myself in the cold pond water and edged myself along the shoreline where I gathered some large, low-bush blueberries; I saved enough for my oatmeal in the morning. I was alone on this magnificent pond, and the stillness was only broken on a couple of occasions by two groups of day hikers who passed nearby. I rinsed some clothes and hung them on a line to dry. A light rain interrupted my plans, and I scurried to my tent with the partially dried garments. No complaints ... this had been a great day! (mile 1,943.3)

DAY 171 – August 27, 1997

I departed Eddy Pond at 0620 and made ready for the challenging ascent of the Saddleback Mountains. This mountain range consisted of three landmarks, Saddleback Mountain, The Horn, and Saddleback Junior. Ski developers and environmental groups hotly contested this area of Maine. The later, want desperately to preserve the natural beauty of the ranges. Should the developer's win out, the public will be the ultimate loser.

I would walk above treeline for the greater part of this day. The views were breathtaking, and as I looked back to where I had come from, I marveled at having had such a rare opportunity to soak in the beauty of this vast land. When I came to Orbeon Stream, it was swollen by rains of the past several days. I slowly picked my way over the moss slickened rocks ... one slip and I would have been in big trouble. I guessed that my early childhood years of walking railroad tracks, and hopping rocks on the Little Pigeon River had given me a slight edge in traversing obstacles such as these.

After the crossing, I sat down on a rock to celebrate my successful crossing. The afternoon climb up Lone Mountain was really difficult, and I arrived at Spaulding Mountain Lean-to just as the heavy rain came. I waited out the rain and pitched my tent behind the Lean-to ... its on to Stratton, tomorrow. (mile 1,958.4)

DAY'S 172/73 - August 28-29, 1997

It rained hard all night and I had a sense of dread as I broke camp at 0610. The extra weight of my rain-soaked tent, as well as some clothes, added further burden to the start of this day. Yesterday's climbs had taken the starch out of my sails and today's terrain didn't look any better. I was headed 13.5 miles to Maine 27, where I hoped to hitch into Stratton for a much-needed rest.

I would have to climb Spaulding Mountain, ford South Branch Carrabasset River, and then climb both South and North Crocker Mountains. It continued to rain most of the morning, and looked threatening the remainder of the day; the slick roots and jagged rocks wore me down by 1000. I was determined to reach Stratton before day's end. The over-sixty crowd was beginning to thin; first it was *Paratrooper,* and now I heard that *Possessed* had fallen and separated a shoulder somewhere on this stretch of the AT.

As I wound my way off Spaulding Mountain, I could see the raging Carrabassett River below. I knew in a heartbeat that no hiker would be able to wade through the turbulence that I could spot from the position that I held on Spaulding Mountain. I began to fear that I would not be able to cross the river, thus delaying Stratton for another day. As I made my descent, I was filled with dread ... seemed like I would never reach the river basin, although I could tell that I was getting close by the sound of rushing water. Much to my relief, the trail maintenance crews had done their job. Three fallen logs had been securely placed across the river. As I slowly inched my way across the walkway, I could hear the boulders cracking against one another, as the sheer force of the raging water propelled them downstream. It took me some time to reach the other side; I was more than a little cautious, as I anticipated every step. When I reached the other side, I took a pack-off break, and gave thanks for my safety. The number of times that I had felt protected by a higher power was now so numerous that I had difficulty in recalling them all. Although Stratton was my goal for the day, I began to develop a contingency plan to set up in a sag between South and North Crocker Mountains.

I supposed that having made it across the Carrabassett River gave me a new lease on life. I arrived at Maine 27 around 1330, and caught a ride into Stratton, 40 minutes later. I immediately checked in at the White Wolf Inn, where I claimed the last available room. I showered and went to the Inn's restaurant, where I enjoyed a much-earned cheeseburger and fries. Next, it was off to the Post Office for my mail drop, and then some much-needed laundry. I returned to my room to sort my food items, when I heard someone say, "Hey, Reveille!" It was none other than Earl Towne from Andover ... he had slacked some hikers to Stratton, and had picked up *The Spice Girls*, *Young-man*, and *Sleepy* on his way into town. He had dropped my trail mates off at the Stratton Motel, where they got the last available bunk spaces at the hostel. *Spam* and *Smoke'n* were not so fortunate, and were hunting a place for the night when I last saw them. Earl gave me an update on *Paratrooper* ... he was slack packing northward on the AT, and still had lots of pain. Earl indicated that he had pretty much decided that if he made it to Katahdin, it would have to be without his usual pack. Maybe he would reach his destination after all; I hoped and prayed that he would stick to slacking for the remainder of his journey.

Later, I called the Towne's back in Andover and spoke with *Paratrooper* ... he seemed in fairly good spirits, but reported much pain in his shoulder and chest ... if anyone can work through pain, he can. I shopped for a few snack items and some film ... then it was off to a prime rib dinner at the Inn. I relished every bite and told myself just how much I deserved such delicacy. During dinner, I ran into three southbound hikers who had flip-flopped somewhere above New York, traveled to Maine, and were now headed back to where they had departed the trail.

I returned to my room and washed my dirt-splattered tent in the bathtub; I had a real mess for a while. I hung the items over the railing of the porch to dry ... fat chance! Around 2000, a major storm blew through and drenched everything. I decided to stay another day in Stratton with the express intent of just kicking back and resting. I had developed a bad habit of running and running to get thing done on my days off ... sometimes, I questioned the necessity of all of the chores that I set out to accomplish.

Maine was beginning to take its toll on all of us hikers. Word was out that *Sandal Man* was hurting so badly that he was going to have to come off the trail for 2-3 days of total rest. Knowing that I still had the "hundred-mile wilderness" ahead didn't do much to lift my spirits. I stayed to myself, as I really didn't feel like talking trail with the others. The next day, as previously vowed, I lounged around town ... took some pictures ... shopped for some gift items for Josephine ... and just kicked back. (mile 1,971.8)

DAY 174 – August 30, 1997
Following a pancake breakfast at the Inn, I walked to the outskirts of this little "Northern Exposure" town, and began hitching a ride back to the trailhead. After a few minutes, a gentleman by the name of Mike Sheridan stopped to pick me up. He was driving a pickup truck, and it was obvious that he was in the construction business. He gave me his business card, and dropped me off where I had left the trail two days ago.

I was now out ahead of the others who would be departing Stratton later in the day. Around 0930, I was pleasantly surprised when *Sir Lancelot* caught up with me; we walked the Bigelow Mountain range together in a driving rain. I was beginning to wonder if the state of Maine ever experienced a ray of sunshine. The wind and rain made for a dismal day of walking ... we put in at Safford Notch Campsite ... not much of a campsite. We ended up tenting next to each other on what was designated as a single site. There was absolutely no level ground on which to throw another tent. Believe me, things were really bad when two seasoned tent campers like us, could not find an alternate site to pitch another tent. On a positive note ... there was a relatively new privy that had been built by a trail maintenance crew. We had to cook our evening meals inside our tent flaps as it was raining steady at 1730. The rains continued well into the night and we knew that we would be packing up wet in the morning. (mile 1,983.0)

DAY 175 – August 31, 1997
We left camp at 0800 and the weather was fairly good ... no rain for a change; water seemed to have saturated everything about us. Today, we would cross Little Bigelow Mountain and Roundtop Mountain, the last big mountain before reaching Mt. Katahdin. The early afternoon weather was much better and we actually saw some sunshine.

We arrived at West Carry Pond Lean-to around 1630 and set up our tents in much better conditions than last evening. *Young-man* and *Sleepy* would come in later and set up near the pond. *Sleepy* had this thing about tenting near the water, and he rarely passed up an opportunity. We learned that *The Spice Girls* were about a day behind, and planned to catch up with the rest of the pack before we reached Harrison's Pierce Pond Camp; we would be there tomorrow as we were only 10.4 miles out. (mile 1,994.5)

DAY 176 – September 1, 1997
    I left camp ahead of the others ... on the trail at 0620 and headed to Pierce Pond Lean-to. As usual, it rained during the night, and light drizzle hung around much of the morning. The trail bordered the many ponds and lakes in this area. We were beginning to become accustomed to the shrill calls of the loons that made their home in this area. While the terrain was not too steep, the trail presented us with the challenge of walking through marshes, intertwined with gnarled, twisted roots. At times, it seemed as if the roots reached out to purposely grab the unsuspecting hiker.
    I slipped and sloshed my way through the next 10 miles. I arrived at Pierce Pond Lean-to around 1115. I found a suitable tenting area just above the lean-to that overlooked Pierce Pond. By mid-evening, all the gang had arrived with the exception of *The Spice Girls,* and they arrived later; they set up camp on the other side of the pond. The rest of us made our way to Harrison's Pierce Pond Camp, where we placed our breakfast orders for the next day, and returned to swim in the pond.
    The sun came out at intervals, and we all gloated in having reached mile 2,004.7 of our journey. We could feel a real sense of camaraderie, as we were now banded together for the final drive to Mt. Katahdin. None of us said much, but we all understood that it was important for us all to make the final climb together. I reworked my itinerary ... I figured 7-8 days to Katahdin once we reached Monson, ME ... now, only three days out! A big day tomorrow ... we will cross the renowned Kennebec River. (mile 2,0004.7)

DAY 177 – September 2, 1997
    We departed camp at 0700 and walked to the Harrison's Pierce Pond Camp for the much-awaited breakfast. *The Spice Girls* decided to bypass the breakfast and went ahead to the Kennebec River, where we would link up with them later in the morning. When we arrived, the Harrison's 8 year-old daughter, Amie, greeted us. She was a real doll and mature beyond her tender years. She invited us to set on the porch while our breakfast was being prepared. In a short while, we were invited in, and found our places around a long table. The interior of the lodge-like dinning area was decorated with trophies that hung over the mantle, as well as on the walls. The Harrison's Camp is well known to avid outdoorsmen who come to the area to fish and hunt.
    Amie was our waitress, and she proudly brought the food that her father was preparing in a nearby kitchen. Our fish camp breakfast consisted of the

following: 12 pancakes, 2 eggs, 3 sausage links, juice, and coffee ... what a feast! We enjoyed Amie as much as we did the food, and we all left her a tip for the grand service. Following some pictures, we made our way back to the AT where we had stowed our pack in some underbrush ... a practice that we had shunned on the trail, but at this very remote site, we felt comfortable in doing so.

We set out for the 3.3-mile walk to the Kennebec River crossing ... the most dangerous river crossing on the trail, due to the rapid rise and surge of water regulated by an upstream dam. In 1985, a female hiker drowned while attempting to cross the river; she had been swept under by the current while struggling to free herself from her pack. Since that time, a ferry service, in the form of a single canoe, operated during the heavy traffic season ... the fee was $10., and well worth it.

We headed a short distance to Caratunk, where we would gather at the only country store in town for resupply. As usual, we all consumed a pint of B&J ice cream and plenty of sodas. It was here that I repacked, and in so doing, laid my pack rain cover and a honey bun on the telephone booth outside the store. I did not discover my mistake until I unpacked for the evening. I felt so perplexed knowing that I would surely need the pack cover with all of the rain that we were experiencing ... not to mention that soft, delicious honey bun. I still couldn't believe that I walked away and left it.

I was the first to leave the store, and I arrived at Pleasant Pond Lean-to before 1400. I boycotted the lean-to, and found a level spot just off the trail leading to Pleasant Pond. *Sir Lancelot* came in and set up nearby; no rain today, and that was quite a treat, in and of itself. The rest of the gang came in by mid-afternoon, and most stayed in the shelter. After everyone was settled in, we walked down to Pleasant Pond, and sat around the lake just soaking up some sun.

Smoke'n left the trail at Caratunk, as this marked the completion of his 2,000-mile journey. He had begun his journey at Mt. Katahdin and walked to Caratunk where he flip-flopped to Springer Mountain, and then made his was back to Caratunk. *Spam* had been his constant trail companion, and now he seemed to be throwing in with us. We all knew that at day's end, we were only two days out of Monson. That could mean only one thing ... the "100-mile wilderness," that would lead us to the base of Mt. Katahdin. (mile 2,014.4)

DAY 177 – Preparing to cross the Kennebec River near Caratunk, Maine.

DAY 178 – September 3, 1997

I broke camp ahead of the others, and headed for Moxie Pond, some 12.3 miles ahead. It had rained all night, and the trail was running full of water … two hard climbs, and then the usual slippery downhills to the campsite. *Young-man* came in behind me, and we both selected our tent sites beyond the lean-to. The shrill echoes of loons were now becoming commonplace; we all seemed to listen with interest for any changes in their calls. I soon realized that I was out of fuel when I attempted to fire my stove for the evening meal … *Young-man* to the rescue; he and *Sleepy* had packed extra fuel, and they seemed glad to share some with me.

We all got together during the evening rain shower, and reworked our final schedule that would carry us through to our destination …or, at least, we hoped that it would. One thing for sure … we all wanted to make that final climb together, for we had been through way too much hardship for any one of us to be left behind. We settled on an 8-day schedule through the "100-mile wilderness." As we folded for the evening, we could all feel a certain sense of excitement, as tomorrow would find us making last minute preparations at Monson, where most of us would find lodging at Shaw's Hiker Hostel. (mile 2,027.5)

DAY 179 – September 4, 1997

I could feel the spring in my steps, as I departed camp for Monson; the data book indicated a 3.3-mile hike on Maine 15 leading into Monson. *Young-man* passed me as usual, and was already settled in at Keith Shaw's Hiker Hostel when I arrived around mid-morning. I had met Keith on the trail several days back, as he was letting a hiker off to resume the trail. He is a fixture in this area of Maine, and had welcomed over 18,000 hikers since 1977. He and his wife, Pat, run the hostel with the help of a son, and they were busy refurbishing another house that would expand their capability to handle even more trail people, as well as hunters.

I opted for a private room over a converted barn next to the main house. I had plenty of privacy, as most to the others chose a bunk area over the Shaw's living quarters. I scurried off to the town Post Office, where I picked up a total of three parcels. The large box had come from home, and would be the last that Josephine would have to coordinate. The other two boxes were essentials that I had mailed from Gorham. The last thing that I wanted was to end up short of supplies, as we made final preparation to enter the "100-mile wilderness." *Sir Lancelot, Young-man, Sleepy*, a female south bounder, and I signed up for Pat Shaw's AYCE evening meal; *The Spice Girls* and *Spam* had opted to stay at another hostel run by the Pie Lady. We were all pleased with the roast beef, potatoes, corn on the cob, etc., all topped off with delicious, fresh blueberry pie. As we devoured all of this, Keith would encourage us to eat more … at one point, he stated that, "We didn't eat like thru-hikers." I thought that we did a fair job of food consumption.

I located the town laundry where I met a nice lady while waiting for my clothes to cycle, and she informed me of the town's history. It was hard to imagine that this little village could exist when the older people die out. There was absolutely nothing that would appeal to the younger generation, as there were no jobs except for short, seasonal work at nearby ski lodges. On my way back to the Shaw's, I realized just how fortunate I was to have experienced this, and many other little villages, and towns along the way.

As I readied for bed, my room seemed like a supply room, as every corner was piled with food and empty boxes. I had to return some of the clothing items that Josephine had sent. The heavy, cotton tee shirts with Tennessee VOLS logos would not be appropriate for the rainy weather that lay ahead; I did keep an orange and white kerchief to display when I reached the summit of Mt. Kathadin. It was hard to explain to people back home that even extra ounces add up when you are walking with a pack in excess of 50 lb. I even sent my water filter home, and opted to use iodine tabs the rest of the way. Much to my surprise, my pack weight was only 47 lbs., and that included an eight-day supply of rations. (mile 2,045.5)

DAY 180 – September 5, 1997

The morning began with a breakfast of blueberry pancakes, eggs, bacon, sausage, muffins, juice, and coffee. Shoney's, eat your heart out! This would prove to be the last great breakfast on the AT. *Sir Lancelot* and I were ready to leave following breakfast, and Mr. Shaw drove us back to the trailhead around 0940. At last, we were about to stride headlong on the much talked about "100-mile wilderness."

We would walk in sunshine most of the day, and reached Wilson Valley Lean-to around 1610. The 10.6 miles seemed easy even though we had to ford two rivers before we made camp. By evening, all of the gang had arrived ... we checked our itineraries and noted that we were scheduled for a 17-mile day for tomorrow. (mile 2,056.1)

> The "100-mile wilderness" is a formidable stretch, as there are no outlets for resupply; that is not to say that one can't arrange for food drops along one of the many forest service roads that bisect the trail. Seasoned thru-hikers normally carry an 8-10 day supply of provisions to get them to Abol Bridge. For most of us, the "wilderness" would be our last serious challenge, and we chose to go with an 8-day supply of food. There are many streams to ford, and one should expect to hike in soggy boots, and rain drenched gear.

DAY 180 – Preparing to enter the "100-mile wilderness."

DAY 181 – September 6, 1997

I was up and on the trail at 0618. I dreaded the steep ascents and descents that were ever-present in these closing days. I walked hard and arrived at Chairback Gap Lean-to at 1540. I had to take my boots off and ford another river … seems now to be a daily event. *Young-man* and I were the only two in at 1800. People are dragging and hurting … me too! Some want to do shorter mileage tomorrow, as we have several big climbs … more rain expected tonight. Tent sites are becoming difficult to find, but I opted to settle on rocky, uneven ground to avoid another night in a trail shelter. I can't remember my last night in a trail shelter … seems like a long time ago. (mile 2,071.7)

DAY 181 – This was the trail that left us exhausted
at day's end.

DAY 182 – September 7, 1997

When I departed Chairback Gap Lean-to the weather was very threatening. It sprinkled at times making the roots and rocks even more difficult to traverse. I forded Pleasant River early in the morning, and headed straight up to Carl A. Newhall Lean-to, where I shared my lunch with a chipmunk.

I moved ahead to Sidney Tappan Campsite, another two-mile climb. I located a good spring, and noted that the sun came out for a brief period of time before giving way to a bleak, gray overcast sky. I felt waterlogged … just like my pack and all its contents. I was having to make the best of using my poncho to cover both me and my pack… still can't believe that I left my pack cover, and that delicious honey bun laying on top of the phone booth back at Caratunk! I've got to get over that honey bun! *Young-man* and I were the first in … others followed … 76.8 miles to go! (mile 2,081.6)

DAY 182 – Weathering the rain, wind, and fog on Avery Peak.

DAY 183 – September 8, 1997

I left camp at 0630 heading for White Cap Mountain, the last really big climb before Katahdin. It rained most of the day, but we were afforded some views from atop White Cap. We spotted what we thought to be Mt. Katahdin, but at this juncture, we were readily acceptable to recognizing any distant peak, as the apex of our long journey.

The remainder of the day was spent descending the mountain, and walking over some delightful rolling grades ... it seemed a long 17.1 miles to Copper Brook Falls Lean-to. On our way, we passed East Branch Lean-to. This would be the shelter that the Towne's helped construct. They had met on the AT and were later married at this very shelter. The Towne's trail names were, *Honey* and *Bear*. I thought of *Paratrooper*, and wondered how he was managing the trail now that the Towne's were assisting him on his way to Katahdin. It was here that *Young-man* had spotted a cow moose and her calf, lazily grazing in the shallows of Pleasant River; for once, I captured this Kodak moment.

It was 1550 when *Young-man* and I made camp. *Sir Lancelot* and *Sleepy* followed; *The Spice Girls* were lagging behind, as they decided to do a short day while the rest of us forged ahead. They have lots of spunk, and no doubt will catch up to us before we reach Baxter State Park. At day's end, I reveled in the fact that this would be my last Monday sleeping on the trail, and the last 17-mile day of my journey. These facts seemed to energize me, and made me forget the utter misery of the daily rains, and slippery footing. I lowered my head, and just walked knowing that the end of the trail was only days ahead. (mile 2,100.6)

DAY 184 – September 9, 1997

I left camp at 0608. Just as I folded my tent and was ready to insert it in my pack, I noticed a shadowy figure moving away from the shelter below me. Who could possibly be on the trail before me? I hurriedly stowed my tent, and set out to learn more about the person ahead of me. In a short while, I spotted a hiker who was eating a breakfast bar along the side of the trail. Glory be ... of all people ... it was *Sleepy*, who really got a kick out of beating *Reveille* out on the trail. The others were also amused at this happening, as *Sleepy* was the very last person that one would expect to accomplish this feat.

It began to drizzle and did not let up the entire day ... what a bummer, this Maine weather. It will rain for sure when we climb Mt. Katahdin on September 13th. I walked 15 miles and put in early at the south end of Nahmakanta Lake. There was not much to do except lay in my tent and listen to the pelting rain ... the site did have a new privy ... too early to cook, so I snacked. The others, except for *The Spice Girls,* came in and pitched their tents in the rain. *Sir Lancelot* was almost run down by a large bull moose while staking out his tent site; that would really have capped off the day. I just wanted this day to pass so that I'd be one day nearer to finalizing this journey ... only 40.9 miles to go! (mile 2,119.5)

DAY 185 – September 10, 1997

Rain ... rain ... and more rain ... all night and all day! This would perhaps be one of the most miserable days since north Georgia, when it seemed that the rain and cold would turn me back. The only difference now, was that nothing, short of death, could turn me back! I found myself counting hours instead of days to put this adventure behind me. The ever-present roots and rocks made every step an adventure, as I slipped and slid my way down most of the steep slopes. I was determined to put in early this day in order to get out of the elements.

I arrived at Rainbow Stream Lean-to by 1330, and set up camp on a hill behind the shelter. I cooked a double dinner ... I'll eat my way through the remainder of this trail, as I still have ample food to get me to Baxter State Park. By mid-afternoon, we were all in, including *The Spice Girls*. We were glad that they had caught up, as we were now only two days out of Daicey Pond Lean-to at the foot of Mt. Katahdin ... only 30.2 miles away! (mile 2,130.2)

DAY 186 – September 11, 1997

I departed at 0615 and made my way across the slippery log footbridge that spanned Rainbow Stream, directly in front of the shelter. The fog was rising from the stream, as I cautiously inched my way forward on the single log ... one slip here, and my day would be ruined.

Sir Lancelot planned to meet a close friend from his hometown in Cherryfield, Maine. Pete was a scoutmaster and civic leader, who also served as a feature writer for the town's weekly newspaper. I set a brisk pace, as I headed towards Abol Bridge Campground, just outside the park boundary. As usual, it was raining, and the trail was a soggy mess ... roots ... roots ...rocks ...rocks ... with a few climbs. I wanted off the trail so badly that I could hardly wait to reach the store at Abol Bridge, and stuff myself with all the pastries and milk that I could possibly consume.

When I arrived at Hurd Brook Lean-to, I met Pete, who was waiting for his friend, and mine, *Sir Lancelot*. I rested a spell, and ate the orange that Pete offered me before moving ahead. I could hardly believe my eyes when I reached the hardtop road that would lead me to the Penobscot River and the Abol Bridge Campstore. It was only 1230 and I was through for the day. The lady who managed the store gave me directions to a state run camping area approximately 100 yards up the road. She indicated that the ranger seldom visited the site and that we would not be charged a fee if he did not come around.

I consumed some microwave food before departing to locate my tent site. I returned to the store, and directed the others to the camping area. At day's end, *Young-man*, *Sleepy*, *Spam*, and I were settled in at the edge of the Penobscot River. We built a fire from driftwood in an attempt to counter the damp chill that always seemed to hang around. *Sir Lancelot* stayed in the commercial campground with his friend, Pete; *The Spice Girls* also opted for the commercial site with showers. Tomorrow we will walk a short 7.7 miles to Daicey Pond Lean-to, where I will chalk up another birthday. (mile 2,145.2)

DAY 187 – September 12, 1997

We broke camp and returned to the camp store for coffee and pastries; it was raining, and I purchase another poncho before setting out for Baxter State Park and Daicey Pond Lean-to. I seemed to be much less concerned about the dismal weather, as I knew that these days were numbered. I walked most of the way with *Sleepy*, as his hiking partner, *Young-man*, was out in front. The trail wound alongside Katahdin Stream that was swollen by days of constant rain that plagued us all the way through the "100-mile wilderness." I was second in behind *Young-man* and set up my tent in the pines beside one of the dual lean-tos.

I walked back to the Ranger Station where I registered, and looked about the area. As I made my way back to the lean-to, my thoughts were directed to tomorrow's final climb and the flight home. The others arrived by noon, and the air was filled with excitement, as we all eagerly anticipated tomorrow's climb. We made final entries in the shelter log ... mostly platitudes depicting the most pleasant memories of our journeys. My final entry alluded to the fact that the Holy Spirit had guided me throughout the 2,000 mile journey and I reminded all to thank their Higher Power, whatever that might be, for safe passage throughout this very long journey. With the excitement surrounding tomorrow's climb, I almost forgot that this day was my 61st birthday. (mile 2,152.9)

DAY 188 – Baxter State Park, at the foot of Mt. Katahdin.

DAY 188 – September 13, 1997 (THE CLIMB)

The morning began at 0500, with me giving wakeup calls to all; most were already awake in anticipation of the "climb." The weather forecast came in from the Ranger Station ... "cloudy with afternoon thunder showers." I left camp at 0608 for the 2.4-mile walk to Katahdin Stream Campground, where we would all begin the final 5.2-mile ascent of Mt. Katahdin. I walked the trail that Josephine and I had walked last October ... it felt good knowing that she had been here, and even walked the first 1.5 miles of the trail leading to the summit of Mt. Katahdin.

We signed in at the Ranger Station and were ready to climb at 0815. I removed all non-essential gear from my pack, and stuffed it with my large plastic bag, snacks, and rain gear. I had carried my pack every step of the way from Georgia, and was not about to make the climb without it! The day was warm and very humid ... I soon shed some outerwear, and moved ahead of *Sir Lancelot* and Pete. The first three miles were not so bad, and I noticed a lot of day hikers on the trail. At the three-mile mark, it was hand-over-hand climbing, as we scaled huge boulders ... some had metal tongs imbedded for handholds.

Once we had traversed the mid-portion of the mountain, the trail became much less treacherous, as the footing improved. The sky began to show signs of clouds, and the wind picked up before I reached the summit at 1040. Much to my surprise, there were at least 10-15 day hikers already perched on the summit. I made my way to the sign marking the end of the trail for all of us. I knelt for a moment of thanksgiving upon touching the sign. I felt peace ... no sadness ... no overpowering jubilation. *The Spice Girls* were tearful with joy, and *Nutmeg* kissed me on the cheek as I congratulated her and *Ginger* on their accomplishment. I reminded them of their prediction way back in Damascus, VA. Sure enough, here we were, all standing together at the end of our journey. We had our pictures taken at the famous signpost that marked the end of the trail.

The skies were looking ominous, as dark clouds began to gather. I decided to depart ahead of the other's, who were still celebrating on the summit. The rain began at 1520, as I made my descent from atop Katahdin's 5,267-foot peak. No more than 30 minutes into my descent, a fierce thunderstorm hit with pelting rain and hail. As lightening flashed and thunder cracked, the thought of not making it off this mountain occurred to me. A day hiker ahead of me gave out a loud shriek following a nearby lightening strike. She had received an electrical charge that did little more than frighten her for the rest of the downward journey. At times, she would stop dead in her tracks upon hearing thunder, and the accompanying lightening that lit up the sky. Everyone ahead of me kept a good pace; a few hikers took cover beneath overhanging rocks, and that was more dangerous than moving forward. It seemed to take longer on the descent ... I could only think of one thing ... reaching the bottom in one piece.

I arrived at the Ranger Station at approximately 1700, and one of the first people that I saw was *Kampfire*. I had heard that he was in the area offering assistance to us thru-hikers, as he had done all the way from Georgia. He asked if I wanted a ride to Millinocket. I gladly accepted his offer, as did the British couple that had camped with us at Daicey Pond Lean-to. He dropped us off at a motel where I showered, did my laundry and ate until I passed out for the evening. (mile 2,160.4)

September 14, 1997

I met *Kampfire* and two other thru-hikers for breakfast; he then shuttled us to Bangor, where I would spend my final night in the great state of Maine. I slept lightly, as the excitement of the next day's flight to Knoxville, Tennessee was ever-present on my mind. Altogether, my senses seemed numbed, and little did I know that it would take months before I would fully appreciate the totality of this experience.

"I think I'll go home now." - Forrest Gump

DAY 188 – "Reveille," atop Mt. Katahdin, Maine.

The Climb

The path that lay before me,
At first it seemed a dream.
With cautious steps it took me,
O'er rocks, hill, and stream.

Onward, always upward,
Thru valleys, peaks, and dale.
Tho' tired, weary, and discouraged,
I knew I would prevail.

Each mountain ever higher,
Perish the thoughts of retreat.
Got to keep a'going
Can't give in to defeat.

When I felt most discouraged,
An act of kindness came my way.
To make me ever thankful,
For the blessings of the day.

Atlas, my goal within my grasp,
I climbed that mountain with the best.
Sweet victory, mine at last,
With God's help, I've passed the test.

- James Richardson

145

EPILOGUE

Adjusting to the "real world" is something that varies by individual. I can only speak of my adjustment, and some of the surprises that it brought. I went through a decompression period, whereas I talked about the trail incessantly; this did not set well with my wife. My biorhythms were out of touch with this new world, and they weren't about to change until they were good and ready! I continue to awaken at 0445 and believe it or not, I still had oatmeal for breakfast, but gladly dispensed with the instant coffee. As for the remainder of the day, I consumed everything in sight, as I needed to regain most of the 26 lb. that I had lost over the past six months.

When I went to my doctor for a check up, my total cholesterol count was 204; it was 263 prior to beginning the trail. I had discontinued my medication shortly after I began the trail in March. I had been plagued with chronic lower back pain over the years, but now had very little discomfort due to the strengthening of by abdominal muscles. It's amazing what carrying a 53 lb. pack for 2,160 miles can do for chronic back pain.

I suppose that my dressing-down caused my wife the most grief. I had hiked for so long in shorts, and tee shirts, that wearing long pants and collared shirts made me feel like I was smothering. I won't go into detail about her reaction to my wearing a dew rag when I mowed the lawn. That head cover had protected me from deer flies, gnats, mosquitoes, sweat bees, hornets, and all manner of flying insects for so long that it was still a part of me. It would be months, rather than weeks, before I settled back into the routines that existed prior to beginning the trail.

The local newspaper printed a feature article about my trail experiences and this led to several church and civic organizations requesting presentations. I have compiled a list of questions most often asked:

• **Why did you decide to hike the AT?** It took a while for me to settle on a single reason, but it all boiled down to "the personal challenge" thing. Sort of like, "the reason to climb a mountain ... because it is there."

• **Would you consider hiking the entire AT again?** I never deliberated long on this response. While I have gone back for some section hikes in southwest Virginia, I would find it very difficult to muster the mental toughness necessary for another venture on the trail. Having experienced the hardships, and knowing what to expect would probably be my downfall should I attempt the AT a second time.

- **How much did your pack weigh?** My average weight was around 53 lb. There were times when I exceeded that weight, and only once did I get my pack weight down to 47 lb. prior to entering the "100 mile wilderness" in Maine.

- **How many pairs of boots did you wear out?** My first pair of boots took me to Harpers Ferry, WV (1,000 miles). My second pair blew-out after another 600 miles; the rugged, rocky terrain in PA caused the inner sole cushioning on one boot to deteriorate, and I replaced them in Manchester Center, VT. I was now on my third pair of boots, and they would take me all the way to Mt. Katahdin, ME.

- **What did you eat and how did you get your food?** My basic breakfast food consisted of two packs of instant oatmeal with instant coffee; occasionally I would be able to add a fried pie or honey bun. Lunch consisted of peanut butter, squeeze cheese, and crackers; I carried small packets of powdered fruit punch for the mid-day break. The evening meal was always the heavy calorie meal. For the most part, it consisted of beans and rice, laced with a 3 oz. can of chicken, or ham. Raman Noodles and Mac & Cheese were alternatives, but I seldom ate the later. Chocolate chip cookies and Snicker Bars were always a good fill-in. I was never a fan of most power bars, as they were too pasty for my taste; I did like Cliff Bars, and purchased them whenever possible. It seemed that we could never get enough fat in our diets to satisfy the enormous amount of calories that we burned each day. Most of our snack food contained more saturated fat than any health conscious person would entertain.

  I obtained most of my food from grocery outlets in towns near the trail. Country stores in isolated communities saved the day on more than one occasion. Some hikers relied primarily on "mail ahead packages," that were sent to designated Post Offices near the trail. I relied on this method on 4-5 occasions, primarily in VT, NH, and ME. Naturally, I took advantage of restaurant food on every occasion when I would come off the trail for resupply. It seemed that sausage and pancake breakfasts, and double cheeseburgers topped the list of my most sought after off-trail foods. Oh yes, cookies, milk, and Ben & Jerry's ice cream were always at the top of my "got to have" list.

- **Did you stay in trail shelters and what were they like?** For the most part, I stayed in shelters only out of necessity. It was required in the Great Smoky Mountain National Park, the Shenandoah National Park, and parts of New Hampshire. Most, if not all, trail shelters were mice infested. That posed a two-fold problem. The mice would sometimes chew through backpacks in search of food, and scamper about during the night, often over your sleeping bag, and sometimes in your hair. If that wasn't enough to harden one against staying in shelters, there was always the threat of contracting Hantavirus from the mice droppings. I preferred the privacy of my two-person tent, and did so approximately 65 percent of my nights on the AT.

• **What are hostels?** Hostels are overnight accommodations sponsored by churches, communities, and privately run enterprises. They provide basic sleeping arrangements varying from a cot, to a mattress, to a wooden platform, to the floor; some offered kitchen privileges, and shower facilities. I stayed in hostels on 16 occasions during my journey. With rare exceptions, those who sponsor these arrangements, do so with a sincere commitment to enable the weary hiker to recover for the next day's journey.

• **What kinds of animals did you encounter along the trail?** I saw countless deer, wild turkeys, grouse, a Peregrine falcon, bald eagles, loon, moose, and a bobcat; I did not see a single black bear although other hikers reported their presence, especially in the Shenandoah National Park.

• **What about snakes?** I saw only one poisonous snake during my journey, and that was a diamondback rattlesnake in PA. If another hiker had not pointed out the snake to me, I would probably have passed it by. Some hikers reported seeing copperhead snakes. I did run across a fair share of black snakes and at least one rat snake.

• **Weren't you afraid to be on the trail by yourself?** Although there were days when I would walk without seeing another person, this was not the norm. When I began the trail in Georgia on my own, it didn't take long to form attachments with fellow thru-hikers. In fact, I climbed the summit of Mt. Katahdin, ME with five hikers that I met in Georgia. While circumstances prevented our hiking together all the way, we hiked VT, NH, and ME, thus completing our journey as a "band of brothers & sisters."

• **Did you carry a gun?** No! It is illegal to carry a concealed weapon on federal lands and I never encountered a situation that would have called for self-defense.

• **Were you ever injured on the trail?** Yes. I took a number of falls, but the two most serious occurred in PA and ME. The first happened on Day 105 just before reaching Port Clinton, PA. During an afternoon thunderstorm, I fell on jagged rocks, and gashed my left elbow and left shin. The deep cut on my shin would have qualified for stitches if I had been near a medical facility. I sutured the cut with super glue, and moved on. The last serious fall that I took was on Day 165, while traversing the Mahoosic Notch near Andover, ME. I fell on rain slickened rocks, and jammed my left wrist and fingers; fortunately my pack absorbed most of the impact and I escaped with only a swollen hand.

- **Where did you get your drinking water?** I filtered all of my water even though some free flowing springs did not need to be filtered. Most of my water came from streams and rivers, and only once did I filter water from a pond.
- **What caused you the most concern while hiking the AT?** In order of concern: (1) hypothermia (2) lightening (3) injury due to falls (4) Giardia (5) snake bite.
- **Did you ever consider coming off the trail?** Yes. On Day 10 in NC, after a miserable, cold, rainy day I questioned why I would want to tolerate such hardship, when I could be eating delicious, home-cooked food and sleeping between sheets. The though stayed with me for the entire day. By the next morning, I had regained by resolve to forge ahead. On at least three other occasions, I seriously considered coming off the trail due to family hardships, back home.
- **What was your most "unusual" experience?** There were so many unusual experiences that I would be hard pressed to choose a single one. I suppose that my overnight stays at the Doyle Hotel in Duncannon, PA, the Graymoor Friary, in NY, and Dartmouth College, NH would top my list.
- **What was your most "rewarding" experience?** Without a doubt, my two-night stay with Earl and Margie Towne in Andover, ME, is one that I will always cherish. Their benevolence and the camaraderie of those hikers that shared this experience with me will forever remain dear to my heart.
- **What was your favorite section of the AT?** Here again, it is difficult to pick a single "favorite" section of the trail. I enjoyed all of southwest Virginia beginning with Mt. Rogers National Park up to the Shenandoah National Park. The rolling pasture land and scenic vistas made it one of my favorites. My favorite state was VT.
- **How many miles per day did you average?** I averaged 12 miles per day. Twenty-four miles was my longest day; my shortest day was less than two miles, due to foul weather while crossing Mt. Washington in NH.
- **How many steps did you take in walking the AT?** At first, I had not a clue regarding this particular question. I have since researched this on the Internet and have arrived at a reasonable answer. According to one website, there are 2,495 steps in a trail mile; thus, I took 5,389,714 steps in completing the official AT mileage.
- **What was the most difficult portion of the AT?** The White Mountains of New Hampshire, also known as the Presidentials, were most difficult. Mt. Washington was especially difficult, due to high winds and frigid temperature. Maine also offered some serious challenges, due to constant rain, swollen rivers,

and difficult terrain.

• **In addition to the official mileage of the AT, how many extra miles did you walk?** There is no way to accurately determine the number of additional miles. I have taken the following factors into consideration in coming up with a reasonable estimate: (1) the added mileage due to misdirection on the AT, (2) the side trails to find water and shelter, and (3) the walks into towns for supplies. A conservative estimate would suggest that I actually walked an additional 400 to 500 miles.

• **How would you categorize the hikers that you met on the AT?** People who hiked the AT in 1997 were a mixed bag. Most were between the ages 20-35 and had taken a break from their jobs or college. A few of the people that I met were retired, and were attempting to live out their dreams of completing the AT. They were by far the most dedicated of those that I met, and were more likely to complete the trail. Most hikers that I met were completing certain sections of the trail while on vacation from their jobs. It is not uncommon for section hikers to take 10-15 years to complete the entire AT. Many hikers start out with good intentions to complete the AT in one season; about 10-15 percent actually succeed in doing so. There is a small minority who tend to hike all, or some portions of the AT every year. These are people with little or no family attachments, and the AT becomes their annual pass time, not to mention their primary social outlet.

• **Did your experiences on the trail change anything about you?** I suppose that I changed my attitude towards people in general. I had decided that the world was pretty much a dog-eat-dog place, and that you had best look out for yourself, as no one else would. When I came off the trail, I no longer believed this to be true, and became much more sensitive to the needs of others. The days of relentless solitude, coupled with the benevolent actions of others, allowed me to reflect on my priorities. I now volunteer with at least three community agencies in addition to our church missions.

• **Do you and fellow hikers get together for reunions?** Yes, on occasions. Trail Days is an annual event held in Damascus, VA, and all but one of my hiking buddies made it to the first reunion in 1998. I try to make the event each year in Damascus and I have attended two similar celebrations in Hot Springs, NC. For the first two to three years following my journeys end, I would frequently look at calendar dates and refer back to my trail notes to see where I was on a particular day. I have passed this stage, but I am frequently reminded of my journey by something as simple as a tree, stream, or changing weather.

EPILOGUE

I still hear from some of my trail mates and have hiked some sections of the Smokies with *Paratrooper,* who resides in western North Carolina. With the help of Earl and Margie Towne, my friend completed the trail despite his injuries. He stood atop Mt. Kathadin on the 24th day of September. One thing for sure, the spring and summer of my 1997 thru-hike on the Appalachian Trail will forever lie fair in my memory.

APPENDICES

-A-
PLANNING GUIDES

There are several planning guides available for the prospective long distance hiker; I utilized the following publications to plan my journey:

The Thru-hiker's handbook, Dan "Wingfoot" Bruce, Center for Appalachian Trail Studies, P.O. Box 525, Hot Springs, NC 28743.

The Thru-hiker's Planning Guide, Dan "Wingfoot" Bruce, Center for Appalachian Trail Studies, P.O. Box 525, Hot Springs, NC 28743.

Appalachian Trail Data Book, Daniel D. Chazin, The Appalachian Trail Conference, P.O. Box 807, Harpers Ferry, WV 25425.

Appalachian Trail Thru-Hikers' Companion, The Appalachian Long Distance Hiker's Association, The Appalachian Trail Conference, P.O. Box 807, Harpers Ferry, WV 25425.

The Appalachian Trail Backpacker's Planning Guide, Victoria and Frank Logue, Menasha Ridge Press, 3169 Cahaba Heights Road, Birmingham, AL 35243.

-B-
EQUIPMENT

This equipment list is what I chose for my journey. If I had it to do over, I would probably go with the same; the exception being, I'd purchase Gore-Tex rain gear.

PACK – MountainSmith, Frostfire II, 6,260 c.i., 5 lbs. 9 oz.	$264.00
RAIN COVER (PACK) – MountainSmith	38.00
TENT – Sierra Designs, Clip Flashlight, 2 person, 3 lbs. 8 oz.	179.00
SLEEPING BAG – Sierra Designs, Lite-N-Up, 20 degree, 3 lbs. 5 oz.	128.00
PAD, Cascade Designs, Therm-A-Rest	11.00
STOVE – MSR WhisperLite Shaker Jet	50.00
POT – REI, Evernew Titanium, 1.3L	45.00
WATER FILTER – SweetWater, Guardian	60.00
BOOTS – ASLO, Gore-Tex, 2 pair	250.00
GAITERS – Outdoor Research	25.00
PANTS – Monterey, water proof	50.00
JACKET – Columbia, Pilot Peak	75.00
VEST – Columbia, fleece	45.00
	$1,220.00

* Equipment costs reflect 1997 dollars; the above items were the main essentials, but did not include all of the items purchased.

-C-
TRAIL TERMS

- **White-Blazer (Purist)** – One who insists on staying on the white-blazed trail, and does not resort to slacking.
- **Blue-Blazer** – One who takes advantage of blue-blazed marked trails on frequent occasions, and in general, is less challenged than those who adhere to the white-blazed trails.
- **Yellow-Blazer** – One who takes unmarked trails to reach a white blazed trail up ahead; a person who walks highway, or accepts a hitched ride to move up the trail, falls in this category.
- **Rainbow-Blazer** – One who utilizes all of the above methods (white-blue-yellow blazing) to reach their desired goal.
- **North-bounder** – One who begins hiking the AT at Springer Mountain, GA.
- **South-bounder** – One who begins hiking the AT at Mt. Katahdin, ME.
- **Flip-flopper** – One who leaves the AT, and travels ahead to another point on the AT, and then resumes hiking back to the point where he/she left the trail. An example would be, the hiker who leaves the AT at Harpers Ferry, WV and travels to Mt. Katahdin, ME, and then hikes back to Harpers Ferry to complete the journey.
- **Slacker (slacking)** – one who hikes without a pack, usually up the AT, but sometimes, southward. This is mostly done with the help of a support person who trails the hiker with a vehicle.
- **Hostel** – a facility on or near the trail where hikers can reconstitute themselves in a trail-friendly environment. The proprietors are usually people who have hiked the AT themselves, or have a penchant for helping hikers reach their goals. These hostels may be in the form of a barn, converted sheds, trailers, homes, etc.
- **B&J** – Ben & Jerry's ice cream; a pint is loaded with more fat calories than any health conscious person would ever want to consume; that is, unless one is hiking 15-20 miles per day on a continuous basis. I have often wondered if anyone has founded a support group for B&J addicted hikers?
- **Trail Magic** – Usually refers to food and drinks left at various places on the AT. I found it easy to expand the meaning of "trail magic" to include

most any benevolent act of kindness, such as an unexpected offer of a ride into the nearest town, or the company of a day hiker to share some conversation. My 2000-mile journey on the AT made me acutely aware that most people continue to be altruistic, and kind-hearted, despite all of the evil and self-centeredness that we hear or see in the media.

- **Yogi-ing** – A thru-hiker technique of acquiring food from non-hikers in a nonchalant manner; wandering through a picnic area where the AT intersects a state park, usually results in an inquiry of, "How far are you going?" That is a perfect lead in to follow on questions, such as, "Where do you get your food?" That is the clincher … the next thing you know, you are eating hamburger and hotdogs with your newfound friends.

-D-
THE THINGS I LEARNED

- **BREAKS** – (Pack-off <u>vs.</u> Pack-on) Pack-off breaks should be limited, as it requires more energy to re-sling and resume; a pack-on break only requires leaning or setting on a supporting structure (log, stump, or ridge).
- **STANDING "8-COUNT"** - When you reach a point where you feel the need for a break, stop in your tracks, and take a brief rest; another component to this, is a simple mind game. Pick out a landmark up ahead, and "make yourself" continue until you reach your goal; then, take "three more steps," so as to move beyond your initial expectation.
- **BY PASSING OBSTACLES** - When you find the trail blocked by large trees (blow downs), instead of attempting to climb over/through, swing yourself under the obstacle; this works only when you have enough clearance for you and your pack.
- **STRING LINES** - After breaking camp, take advantage of the wind and sun to dry your nylon tent, or other gear. String a line during a break, and dry your gear while you reconstitute yourself. No one needs the extra burden of carrying additional ounces as a result of wet gear.
- **FILTERING WATER** - Place the pre-filtering end of the siphoning hose in a canteen cup to avoid taking in silt and debris to the main filtering unit. This will prolong the life of the filters and result in less maintenance.
- **STORING COOKIES/CRACKERS** – Pringles canisters make excellent storage units for those chocolate chip cookies that hikers so desperately crave. Also, store a plastic knife/spoon here to spread your peanut butter, cheese, jelly, etc.
- **COOKING** – Avoid using your stove more than twice each day; boil water for oatmeal and coffee/tea for breakfast and for the main dinner at the end of the day … this meal will consume the greater amount of fuel.
- **WIND BREAK FOR STOVE** – Wrap the aluminum foil wind break around your fuel cell (bottle); this will ensure the cylindrical shape and you'll never have to look through you gear, as it will always be with your heating unit.

- **DEW RAGS** – Bandanas are not just for looking cool …they can keep you cool, and ward off those pesky deer flies and mosquitoes that hone in on your head on a sweltering hot day. Keep one attached to your pack or hiking stick, as well as the one that you wear on your head. During the summer months, drench the rag at every water source … you'll be surprised how refreshing this is.
- **DATA BOOK** – Separate the *Appalachian Trail Data Book* by sections, and have your home base support person mail them at appropriate intervals; no need to lug more than you have to. This, likewise, holds true for other trail guides and maps.
- **MAIL DROPS** – Some thru-hikers utilized mail drops as their primary source of food supply; this requires meticulous planning and a little luck in arriving on schedule, so as to be able to pick up the package during business hours. The packages must be sent, General Delivery, % NAME , City, State, ZIP. I chose to "live off the shelf" (super markets, country stores) for the most part, with less than six mail drops.
- **INSECT REPELLENT & HAND SANITIZER** – Store these two essentials in a side pocket of your pack where you carry your water; they will always available when you need them.
- **SUPER GLUE** – Normally used for boot or nylon patches; I used the glue to suture a leg gash suffered in a fall in PA; it worked as well as sutures and left no scar.
- **INDUSTRIAL STRENGTH PLASTIC BAG** – This is absolutely indispensable; use to carry your wet gear, primarily your tent. "Packing up wet" is an everyday occurrence; top load the wet tentage and dry it later in the day (see STRING LINES).
- **BOILING POT** – Avoid carrying more than a single pot; stow the evening meal (noodles, rice, macaroni, etc.) or (energy bars, pastries, etc.) in the pot in order to save pack space for other essential items.
- **LOST ITEMS** – Be prepared to loose some of your equipment; odds are that you will also find equipment as you move along the trail. Leave notes in the shelter log books regarding lost and found items.
- **SANDWICH BAGS** – Always break your food items out of cardboard packaging; some even broke their Raman Noodles out of the original packages. Save the used bags to collect your trash such as foil packaging, tin cans, paper, or any other disposable. Place this "garbage container" in the very top of your pack and dispose in a proper receptacle. **REMEMBER**: "Pack it in; Pack it out."

"Therefore I tell you; do not worry about your life, what you will eat or drink; or about your body, what you will wear. Is not life more important than food, and the body more important than clothes? Look at the birds of the air; they do not sow or reap or store away in barns, and yet your heavenly father feeds them. Are you not much more valuable than they?"

NIV - Matthew 6:25-26

Printed in the United States
210782BV00001B/81/A

9 781591 137122